魏 剑 峰

和

他 的 猫

高频
口语表达
200
例

英语口语必备

小蓝书

魏剑峰——

主编

上海交通大学出版社
SHANGHAI JIAO TONG UNIVERSITY PRESS

内容提要

本书是一本通过口语训练提升英语水平的图书。全书共包括社会、媒体与广告、科技、健康、教育、工作、环保、政府、个人品质和文化等十大主题200个实用表达。针对每个表达，本书不仅给出句型解析，还提供实用语境，便于读者学以致用。本书适合中等水平及以上英语学习者使用。

图书在版编目（CIP）数据

英语口语必备小蓝书：高频口语表达200例 / 魏剑峰主编. — 上海：上海交通大学出版社，2024.1
ISBN 978-7-313-30119-2

Ⅰ. ①英…　Ⅱ. ①魏…　Ⅲ. ①英语—口语—自学参考资料　Ⅳ. ①H319.9

中国版本图书馆CIP数据核字（2024）第005184号

英语口语必备小蓝书：高频口语表达 200 例
YINGYU KOUYU BIBEI XIAOLANSHU: GAOPIN KOUYU BIAODA 200 LI

主　　编：魏剑峰
出版发行：上海交通大学出版社　　　地址：上海市番禺路 951 号
邮政编码：200030　　　　　　　　　电话：021-64071208
印　　制：苏州市越洋印刷有限公司　　经销：全国新华书店
开　　本：880mm×1230mm　1/32　　印张：7
字　　数：206 千字
版　　次：2024 年 1 月第 1 版　　　　印次：2024 年 1 月第 1 次印刷
书　　号：ISBN 978-7-313-30119-2
定　　价：48.00 元

英语口语必备小蓝书

前　言

　　对中国学生来说，英语口语是个老大难问题。不少人做了大量的阅读和听力练习，但说起英语还是磕磕绊绊，头脑一片空白。造成这一问题的原因主要有两个：一个是缺乏开口练习的机会，另一个是素材积累不足。

　　口语技能在很大程度上属于"肌肉记忆"，需要大量的开口练习才能熟练掌握。如果只是一直做阅读和听力练习而不主动开口说英语，那么"输入"再多也难以转化为一口流利的英语。素材积累也是一个问题。一些同学虽然读了不少文章，但没有对其中好的素材进行复习总结，也没有背诵好词、好句的习惯，这导致能真正记住和应用的内容非常少。

　　有鉴于此，提升英语口语也要从这两个方面入手。一方面要保证每天开口说英语，坚持下来形成肌肉记忆。另一方面要总结积累实用的口语素材，对于好的表达可以背下来，这样更加容易应用。

　　那么，什么样的素材值得积累呢？在长期的教研实践中，我发现有一些口语表达在特定主题中的出现频率非常高，这样的表达就值得积累。

　　比如在文化类话题中有一个高频地道短语 pass something down from generation to generation，在讨论传统节日、家族物品

以及传统习俗等话题时，我们都可以用上该短语，表示"将某事物代代相传"。比如：在口语考试中，

考官问你：Do you think cultural traditions are important?

你可以回答：Yes, I think cultural traditions are extremely important because they embody values, beliefs, and practices that have been passed down from generation to generation. They not only serve as a bridge between the past and the present but also provide a sense of identity and belonging, helping us understand who we are and where we come from.

考官问你：Do you have any family traditions?

你可以回答：In my family, we have a tradition of making dumplings together every Chinese New Year. This recipe has been passed down from generation to generation and it's a great way for us to bond and celebrate our heritage.

可以看到，这一短语在文化类话题中有很广泛的应用。其他话题中也有一些类似的表达，比如 want the best for somebody（教育话题）, be in the public interest（政府话题）, reduce somebody's carbon footprint（环保话题）, stay relevant（工作话题）, be a status symbol（时尚话题）等。

这样的口语高频表达我一共整理了 200 个，涵盖健康、教育、环保、社会、科技、政府以及个人品质等常见的 10 类话题。如果你

能熟练掌握这 200 个口语高频表达，那么可以肯定的一点是，你的口语表达流利度将会有一个很大的提升。

这些表达本身包含了很多常见口语题目的回答思路，掌握这些表达能够帮你拓展素材库，在口语中变得有话可说。举个例子，在媒体和广告话题中，有这么一个高频表达: unrealistic body standards（不切实际的身材标准），在阐述媒体和广告的缺点时可以用上该短语。目前不少广告里面的模特往往具有完美身材，这容易树立不切实际的身材标准，让普通人感到焦虑以及不自信。在口语考试中如果有考官问你广告有哪些缺点，你就可以回答:

One of the disadvantages of advertisements is that they often promote unrealistic body standards. Advertisements, particularly those related to fashion and beauty products, often portray models with perfect skin, hair, and body shape. This can lead to people comparing themselves with these models and feeling inadequate or dissatisfied with their own appearance.

我对书中这 200 个高频表达都给出了详细解析，重点说明这些表达的意思和使用语境。同时，为了让各位同学更好地掌握这些表达的用法，我还为它们编写了具体的使用场景。同时，这些英文使用场景也都配有美音朗读音频，方便各位模仿跟读。

各位同学在阅读本书时可以重点关注自己不熟悉或者觉得有亮点

的表达，然后采取口头造句等方式加深对它们的印象。有时间、有精力的同学还可以背诵书中好的例句和段落。

口语提升是一个长期的过程，关键是要做到多开口以及多积累素材。希望本书能帮你迈出口语精进的第一步。

需要进一步提升写作水平的同学也可以读一读我的另一本图书《英语写作必备小红书：纯正英语句型 300 例》。书中精选了 300个地道的外刊写作句式，并带有详细的解析，掌握这些句式能够帮你写出漂亮的句子。

最后，本书编写过程中因人力、时间和水平有限，错漏不妥之处在所难免。各位可关注我的公众号"英文悦读"，并通过评论留言等形式反馈您的宝贵意见。祝各位学习进步！

魏剑峰

2023 年秋于广州

目　录

社会话题

Part 1

扫一扫, 听录音

01 be stuck in low-paying, unstable work
02 volunteer somebody's time and skills to do something
03 live paycheck to paycheck
04 somebody/something is stigmatized
05 rush hour
06 stay connected with society
07 cut back on something
08 move up the social ladder
09 live a hand-to-mouth existence
10 live beyond your means
11 settle down
12 something is key in addressing the issue of ...
13 life expectancy
14 get on the property ladder
15 provide for somebody
16 start a family
17 nuclear family
18 bond with somebody
19 take care of household chores

01 be stuck in low-paying, unstable work

用法解析

stuck 在这里是形容词，意思是"卡住，困住"，be stuck in low-paying, unstable work 即"被困在低薪且不稳定的工作中"。该短语可以用来描述穷人所处的困境。

实用语境

What do you think are some of the main causes of poverty?
你认为造成贫穷的原因有哪些？

I think one of the main causes of poverty is the lack of access to education and job opportunities. Many people who live in poverty don't have the skills or education needed to get well-paying jobs, so they're *stuck in low-paying, unstable work*. Another cause is the high cost of living, especially in urban areas. Housing, food, and healthcare can be very expensive, making it difficult for people to make ends meet.

我认为造成贫穷的一个主要原因是缺乏教育和就业机会。许多生活贫困的人没有获得高薪工作所需的技能或教育，因此他们只能被困在低薪、不稳定的工作当中（be stuck in low-paying, unstable work）。另一个原因是生活成本高，尤其是在城市地区。住房、食品和医疗非常昂贵，使人们难以维持生计。

02 volunteer somebody's time and skills to do something

volunteer 除了可以当名词表示"志愿者"之外，还可以用作动词，表示"自愿做某事"，短语 volunteer somebody's time and skills to do something 即表示"某人自愿贡献时间和精力去做某事"。

用法解析

What can individuals do to help reduce poverty?
个人可以做些什么来帮助减少贫困？

实用语境

I think individuals can help reduce poverty by supporting organizations that work to address poverty and its causes. They can also *volunteer their time and skills* to help those in need. Additionally, individuals can advocate for policies and programs that aim to alleviate poverty and raise living standards.

我认为，个人可以通过支持那些致力于消除贫困及其根源的组织来帮助减少贫困。他们还可以自愿贡献自己的时间和技能（volunteer their time and skills），帮助那些需要帮助的人。此外，个人还可以拥护那些旨在减轻贫困和提高生活水平的政策和项目。

03 live paycheck to paycheck

 用法解析

paycheck 的意思是"薪水支票，工资"，live paycheck to paycheck 的字面意思是"一份工资花完等下一份工资"，相当于我们说的"月光"。比如：We are living paycheck to paycheck and have no money left over for savings. 我们过着月光生活，没有余钱用来存款。

 实用语境

Do you think it's important for people to save money?
你认为存钱重要吗？

Absolutely. Compared to those who *live paycheck to paycheck*, people who save money are more likely to have peace of mind, because they don't have to constantly worry about financial troubles. Saving money can also help people prepare for unexpected events, such as medical emergencies, job loss, or car repairs.

当然。与那些月光族（live paycheck to paycheck）相比，存钱的人更容易心平气和，因为他们不必总是担心财务问题。存钱还能帮助人们为意外情况做好准备，如生病、失业或汽车维修。

04 somebody/something is stigmatized

该短语的意思是"某事物或某人受到歧视"，在描述像离婚、单身母亲以及种族等话题时经常可以用到该表达。比如：Single mothers often feel that they are stigmatized by society. 单身母亲常常感到自己受到了社会的歧视。

用法解析

Do you think the rate of divorce has increased in recent years?
你认为离婚率在近年来有所上升吗？

实用语境

Yes, the rate of divorce has indeed increased in recent years. This could be due to several factors. Firstly, societal norms have changed significantly over the past few decades. Divorce is no longer *stigmatized* as it used to be, and people are now more aware of their rights and are less likely to stay in unhappy marriages. Additionally, with the rise of social media and dating apps, people may be tempted to explore options outside their marriage.

是的，近年来离婚率确实有所上升。这可能是由几个因素造成的。首先，在过去几十年里，社会规范发生了重大变化。离婚不再像以前那样被污名化（be stigmatized）。人们现在更加了解自己的权利，也越来越不愿意维持不幸福的婚姻。此外，随着社交媒体和约会应用软件的兴起，人们可能会受到诱惑，去探索婚姻之外的选择。

05 | rush hour

用法解析

rush hour 的意思是"上下班的高峰时间，交通拥挤时间"，比如：I got caught in the morning rush hour. 我在早上的交通高峰时间遇上了塞车。要表达"交通高峰期"，还可以说 peak times，比如：Extra buses run at peak times. 交通高峰期加开公共汽车。

实用语境

What are some possible solutions to reduce traffic congestion?
有哪些可能减少交通拥堵的措施?

There are several potential solutions to this problem. One is improving public transportation systems to encourage more people to use them instead of private vehicles. Another way to reduce traffic congestion is by creating more pedestrian-friendly areas or improving road infrastructure. Lastly, flexible working hours or remote work could reduce the number of people commuting at *rush hour*.

这一问题有几种潜在的解决方案。一种是改善公共交通系统，鼓励更多人使用公共交通，而不是私家车。另一种减少交通拥堵的方法是创建更多方便行人的区域，或者改善道路基础设施。最后，灵活的工作时间或远程工作可以减少上下班高峰期（rush hour）的通勤人数。

06 stay connected with society

该短语的意思是"与社会保持连接，不与社会脱节"。
与社会保持连接的方式包括参与志愿活动、上班以
及参加社交活动等，比如：Volunteering in local
community services is an excellent way to stay
connected with society, as it allows individuals to
understand the diverse needs of their community.
在当地社区服务机构做志愿者是与社会保持联系的绝佳
方式，因为这可以让人了解社区的各种需求。

用法解析

How can families contribute to the care of their
elderly members?
家庭成员应该如何为照顾老人做出贡献？

实用语境

Families are often the primary caregivers for elderly
members. They can contribute by ensuring their
physical well-being, providing emotional support,
and helping them *stay connected with society*. It's also
important for families to respect their independence
and involve them in decision-making processes.

家庭成员往往是老年人的主要照顾者。他们可以
通过确保老年人的身体健康、提供情感支持以
及帮助他们与社会保持联系（stay connected with
society）来做出贡献。同样重要的是，家人要尊重
他们的独立性，让他们参与决策过程。

07 cut back on something

用法解析

cut back on something 的意思是"削减，减少（消费、开支等）"，在消费类相关的话题中可以用上该表达。比如：In an effort to save money, some families have decided to cut back on their monthly shopping expenses by buying only essential items. 为了省钱，一些家庭决定减少每月的购物开支，只购买必需品。

实用语境

How does an economic recession impact ordinary people?
经济衰退如何影响普通人？

An economic recession can have profound effects on ordinary people. Job security can be threatened as companies might need to lay off employees to cut costs. This can lead to unemployment, causing a decrease in household income. As a result, people may need to adjust their spending habits, often *cutting back on* non-essential items. In severe cases, some individuals might struggle with affording basic necessities like food and housing.

经济衰退会对普通人产生深远影响。人们的工作保障可能受到威胁，因为公司可能需要裁员以削减成本。这会导致失业，造成家庭收入减少。因此，人们可能需要调整自己的消费习惯，通常会削减（cut back on）非必需品。在严重的情况下，一些人可能难以负担食物和住房等基本必需品。

08 move up the social ladder

ladder 在这里指的是"（在机构、职业或社会中逐渐晋升的）阶梯，途径"，move up the social ladder 即"提升社会阶级"，"社会阶级滑落"则可以说 move down the social ladder。

How important is education in your country?
教育在你们国家有多重要?

Education is highly valued in my country. Many people believe that education is the key to success and a way to *move up the social ladder*. It provides individuals with the knowledge and skills necessary to pursue their desired career and make a decent living.

教育在我们国家受到高度重视。许多人认为，教育是成功的关键，也是提升社会地位（move up the social ladder）的途径。教育为个人提供必要的知识和技能，使他们能够从事理想的职业，过上体面的生活。

09 live a hand-to-mouth existence

用法解析

live a hand-to-mouth existence 的意思相当于"过着手停口停的生活",也即"过着勉强糊口的生活",比如: The worst-paid live a hand-to-mouth existence without medical or other benefits. 收入最低者过着只能勉强糊口的日子,没有医疗补助或其他福利。

实用语境

What are some of the challenges that people face when living in poverty?
生活贫困的人会遇到哪些挑战?

I think one of the biggest challenges that poor people face is the constant struggle to make ends meet. They often *live a hand-to-mouth existence*, meaning that they have just enough money to survive but not enough to save or invest in their future. This can make it difficult for them to break the cycle of poverty and improve their situation. Another challenge is that poor people are more likely to suffer from health problems due to inadequate nutrition and limited access to healthcare.

我认为,穷人面临的最大挑战之一就是不断为生计而挣扎。他们往往过着手头拮据的生活(live a hand-to-mouth existence),这意味着他们只有足够的钱维持生存,却没有足够的钱用来储蓄或投资自己的未来。这使得他们很难打破贫困的恶性循环,改善自己的处境。另一个挑战是穷人由于营养不足以及获得医疗保健的机会有限,因此更容易出现健康问题。

10 live beyond your means

该短语中 means 的意思是"金钱，收入"，比如：I don't have the means to support a family. 我没有钱养家。live beyond your means 即表示"入不敷出"，另一个相对的表达则是 live within your means（量入为出）。

用法解析

Why do people overspend?
为什么人们会花钱超支？

实用语境

I think people overspend for various reasons. Some people do this because they lack basic financial knowledge and budgeting skills, while others may have a tendency to impulse buy. Additionally, social pressure and the desire to keep up with others can also lead people to *live beyond their means*. Unfortunately, this can often result in people running into debt.

我认为人们花钱超支有各种原因。有些人花钱超支是因为他们缺乏基本的财务知识和做预算的技能，而有些人则可能有冲动购物的倾向。此外，社会压力和追随他人的欲望也会导致人们入不敷出（live beyond their means）。不幸的是，这往往会导致人们负债。

11 settle down

用法解析

该短语的意思相当于"定居，安顿下来"，尤其是指买房或结婚后安顿下来，比如：They'd like to see their daughter settle down, get married, and have kids. 他们希望女儿安顿下来，结婚成家，生儿育女。

实用语境

Do you think the concept of marriage is changing in your country?

你认为你们国家的婚姻观念正在发生变化吗？

Yes, I think so. Nowadays, people are getting married later in life and are more focused on their careers and personal development before *settling down*. There is also a growing acceptance of different forms of relationships, such as cohabitation. Overall, I think people are becoming more open-minded about what marriage means and what it can look like.

是的，我是这样认为的。如今，人们结婚的年龄越来越晚，他们在安顿下来（settle down）之前更注重事业和个人发展。人们也越来越接受不同形式的关系，比如同居。总的来说，我认为人们在婚姻的含义和婚姻形式方面的观念越来越开放。

12 something is key in addressing the issue of ...

该短语中的 key 是形容词，而不是名词，意思是"关键的，最重要的"，比如：Good communication is key to our success. 良好的沟通是我们成功的关键。Something is key in addressing the issue of ... 的意思是"某事物对解决……问题至关重要"。

How do you think society can address the issue of domestic violence?
你认为社会应该如何解决家庭暴力问题？

I believe that education and awareness are *key in addressing the issue of* domestic violence. It's important for people to understand what constitutes abusive behavior and to recognize the warning signs of an abusive relationship. There should also be support systems for victims of domestic violence, such as shelters and counseling services.

我认为，教育和意识是解决家庭暴力问题的关键（be key in addressing the issue of）。重要的是，人们要了解什么是虐待行为，并认识到一段虐待关系的警示信号。此外，人们还应该为家庭暴力受害者提供支持，如庇护所和咨询服务。

13 | life expectancy

用法解析

life expectancy 的意思是"（人的）预期寿命"，比如：Life expectancy in Europe has increased greatly in the 20th century. 欧洲人的预期寿命在 20 世纪大幅增长。要表达"预期寿命增长"，可以说 an increase in life expectancy，表示下降则是 a decline in life expectancy。

实用语境

How has the population structure changed in your country in recent years?
近年来，你们国家的人口结构发生了哪些变化？

In recent years, China has seen a significant increase in the proportion of older people. This is mainly due to advances in healthcare and nutrition, which have led to an increase in *life expectancy*. As a result, the population is ageing, and this trend is expected to continue in the coming years.

近年来，中国的老年人口比例显著增加。这主要是由于医疗保健和营养方面的进步导致预期寿命（life expectancy）延长。这导致了人口老龄化加剧，预计这一趋势在未来几年仍将持续。

14 get on the property ladder

property 的意思是"房地产"，比如：Property prices have shot up recently. 最近房地产价格暴涨。get on the property ladder 的意思相当于我们说的"买房上车"。

用法解析

What are some of the challenges young people face when trying to buy their first home?
年轻人在购买首套房时会遇到哪些挑战？

实用语境

I think one of the biggest challenges young people face is the high cost of housing. In many cities, property prices have risen significantly in recent years, making it difficult for young people to *get on the property ladder*. This often means that it'll take a long time for them to save for a down payment, or they may need to borrow money from family or friends. Additionally, the process of getting a mortgage can be complicated and time-consuming, which can be discouraging for first-time buyers.

我认为年轻人面临的最大挑战之一就是高昂的房价。近年来，许多城市的房价大幅上涨，这使得年轻人很难买房上车（get on the property ladder）。这往往意味着他们需要很长时间才能攒够首付，或者他们可能需要向家人或朋友借钱。此外，申请抵押贷款的过程可能既复杂又耗时，这可能会让首次购房者望而却步。

15 provide for somebody

用法解析

该短语的意思是"供养某人，抚养某人"，比如：
Without work, how can I provide for my children?
没有工作，我如何抚养孩子？该短语的一个常见搭配是
provide for somebody's family（养家）。

实用语境

How do you think the economy affects people's daily lives?
你认为经济如何影响人们的日常生活？

The economy can have a big impact on people's daily lives. For example, if the economy is doing well, people may have more job opportunities and higher salaries. However, if the economy is in bad shape, people may lose their jobs and struggle to *provide for* their family. This can cause a lot of stress and uncertainty for them.

经济环境会对人们的日常生活产生重大影响。例如，如果经济环境良好，人们可能会有更多的工作机会和更高的薪水。然而，如果经济环境不佳，人们可能会失去工作，难以养家糊口（provide for）。这会给他们带来很大的压力和不确定性。

16 start a family

注意 start a family 的意思相当于 have children，因此该短语不能简单理解为"成家"，而是要理解为"生小孩"。比如：They want to get married and start a family. 他们想要结婚生小孩。

Why are young people having fewer children?
为什么年轻人越来越少生小孩？

I think there are many factors that contribute to the decline in birth rates. One of them is that more and more women are choosing to pursue higher education and careers, which often leads to them delaying getting married and *starting a family*. Additionally, the cost of child-rearing has increased significantly, making it more difficult for young people to have children.

我认为导致出生率下降的因素有很多。其中之一就是越来越多的女性选择读大学和进入职场，这往往导致她们推迟结婚生小孩(start a family)。此外，养育子女的成本大幅增加，使年轻人更难生育。

17 nuclear family

用法解析

Nuclear family 是指"仅由夫妻与子女组成的核心家庭，小家庭"，与之相对的是 extended family，指包括祖父母和叔叔婶婶等在内的大家庭。

实用语境

How has the size of the family changed in the last few decades in your country?

在过去几十年中，你们国家的家庭规模发生了哪些变化？

In recent decades, there has been a shift from extended families living together in one household to *nuclear families*. As a result, the size of a typical family in my country has decreased to about 3 or 4 people in one home.

近几十年来的一个趋势是从大家庭向核心家庭（nuclear families）转变。这导致的结果是我国一个典型家庭的规模已经缩小到一户人家只有三四个人。

18 | bond with somebody

bond 作动词时可以表示"与某人培养感情，建立互信关系"，比如：Time must be given for the mother to bond with her baby. 母婴之间必须通过时间来培养亲情。

Do grandparents play an important role in the family in your country?
在你们国家，祖父母在家庭中是否扮演了重要的角色？

Yes, grandparents play a very important role in Chinese families. They often act as caregivers for their grandchildren, especially when both parents have to work outside the home. This reduces the burden of childcare for parents, and gives them a chance to *bond with* their grandchildren.

在我国，祖父母在家庭中扮演着非常重要的角色。他们经常充当孙辈的照顾者，尤其是当父母都需要外出工作时。这减轻了父母照顾小孩的压力，也使祖父母有机会与孙辈建立情感联系（bond with）。

19 | take care of household chores

用法解析

household chores 的意思是"家务活"，它也可以说成 domestic chores，take care of household chores 即表示"做家务活"。

实用语境

What are some of the advantages of living alone?
独居都有哪些优点？

One advantage of living alone is that you have complete control over your living space. You can decorate and organize your home however you like, without having to compromise with roommates or family members. Additionally, living alone can provide a sense of independence and self-sufficiency, as you are responsible for managing your own finances, cooking your own meals, and *taking care of household chores*.

独居的一个好处是你对自己的生活空间有控制权。你可以随心所欲地装饰和布置自己的家，而不必向室友或家人妥协。此外，独居还能给你带来一种独立和自给自足的感觉，因为你需要负责自己的财务、自己做饭和料理家务（take care of household chores）。

扫一扫，听录音

媒体与广告

Part 2

01 something is a status symbol
02 promote materialism
03 something is on-trend
04 word of mouth
05 be bombarded with something
06 take something at face value
07 impulse buying
08 feel comfortable in somebody's own skin
09 unrealistic body standards
10 something is blown out of proportion
11 be in the public eye
12 dominate the headlines
13 present something in a positive light
14 somebody has a large following
15 support good causes
16 something brings attention to
17 fit in with somebody
18 personal grooming
19 be appealing to somebody

01 something is a status symbol

用法解析

status symbol 的意思是"身份的象征"，比如：A Rolls Royce is seen as a status symbol. 劳斯莱斯轿车被视为社会地位的象征。像豪车（luxury cars）、名牌服装（designer clothes）以及大房子（big houses）都可以被视为身份地位的象征。

实用语境

Why do people buy luxury products?
为什么人们会购买奢侈品？

I think the reason people buy luxury products like expensive cars and designer clothes is that they are *a status symbol*. They can use luxury products to show off their wealth and social status. For example, some people buy fancy cars because they want to impress others and show that they are financially successful.

我认为，人们之所以购买昂贵的汽车和名牌服装等奢侈品，是因为它们是一种身份的象征（a status symbol）。他们可以用奢侈品来炫耀自己的财富和社会地位。例如，有些人购买酷炫的汽车，是因为他们想给别人留下深刻印象，显示自己经济富裕。

02 promote materialism

该短语的含义是"宣扬物质主义"，在关于媒体和
广告缺点的话题中经常会出现这一说法，比如：
Advertisements on television often promote
materialism, encouraging consumers to buy more
than they need. 电视广告经常宣扬物质主义，鼓励消
费者购买超出自己需求的东西。

用法解析

What do you think are the negative effects of
advertising?
你认为广告的负面影响有哪些？

实用语境

I think one of the negative effects of advertising is
that it can mislead customers by presenting false
information about goods. Another problem is that
advertising often *promotes materialism*. For example,
when we see advertisements for expensive cars
or designer clothes, we are encouraged to believe
that owning these things will make us happy and
successful. This can lead to us spending money on
things we don't really need.

我认为广告的负面影响之一是它可能通过提供虚
假的商品信息误导顾客。另一个问题是广告往往
助长物质主义（promote materialism）。例如，当
我们看到昂贵汽车或名牌服装的广告时，我们会
被鼓励相信拥有这些东西会让我们快乐和成功。
这会导致我们把钱花在并不真正需要的东西上。

03 | something is on-trend

on-trend 的意思相当于 very fashionable，即"流行的，时尚的"，比如：the best place to buy on-trend party clothes 购买时髦的宴会礼服的好地方。意思相似的表达还有 trendy。

Do you think fashion is important?
你认为时尚重要吗？

Yes, I believe that fashion plays a significant role in modern society. Today more and more people are becoming fashion-conscious, and they take pride in keeping up with what's *on-trend*. Fashion allows them to showcase their unique tastes, preferences, and personality traits through the clothes and accessories they choose to wear. It can also help them highlight their best features and boost their confidence.

是的，我相信时尚在现代社会中扮演着重要角色。如今，越来越多的人开始关注时尚，他们以紧跟潮流（on-trend）为荣。时尚可以让他们通过自己选择的服装和配饰来展示自己独特的品位、喜好和个性特征。时尚还能帮助他们突出自己的最大特点并增强自信。

04 word of mouth

word of mouth 是一个固定短语，意思是"口口相传，口碑"，比如：The restaurant does not advertise, but relies on word of mouth for custom. 这家餐馆并没有做广告，而是依靠口碑来赢得顾客。

用法解析

What makes a film successful?
是什么因素能让一部电影取得成功？

实用语境

There are many factors that contribute to the success of a film. A well-written script, engaging characters, and good acting are all important elements. Additionally, effective marketing and positive *word of mouth* can also help to attract audiences. Ultimately, a successful film is one that resonates with its viewers and leaves a lasting impression.

一部电影的成功有许多因素。精心编写的剧本、引人入胜的角色和出色的演技都是重要因素。此外，有效的市场营销和积极的口碑（word of mouth）也有助于吸引观众。归根结底，一部成功的电影应能引起观众的共鸣，并给观众留下深刻的印象。

05 be bombarded with something

用法解析

该短语表示"被……轰炸，被……淹没"，比如：
The office was bombarded by telephone calls. 办公室里电话响个不停。此短语也可以用主动用法 bombard somebody with something，比如：They bombarded him with questions. 他们连珠炮似的向他提问。

实用语境

Do you think people in your country are influenced by consumerism?
你觉得你们国家的人受到消费主义影响吗？

Yes, I believe that consumerism has become a prevalent mindset in my country. People are constantly *bombarded with* messages encouraging them to buy the latest electronic gadgets and fashion items. As a result, many people succumb to the temptation of consumerism and end up buying more than they need.

是的，我认为消费主义在我国已成为一种普遍心态。人们不断受到各种信息的轰炸（be bombarded with），鼓励他们购买最新的数码产品和时尚物品。因此，许多人屈服于消费主义的诱惑，最终购买了超过自己需要的东西。

06 | take something at face value

该短语的意思是"仅凭表象对……信以为真"，比如：
You shouldn't take anything she says at face value.
她的话你绝对不能仅凭表面就信以为真。在涉及媒体信息与独立思考话题时可以用上该说法。

Do you think the media can shape public opinion?
你认为媒体能左右公众舆论吗？

Yes, I think the media play a significant role in shaping public opinion. People often rely on various media platforms, such as television, newspapers, and social media, to gather information and form their views on different matters. However, it's important to approach the information presented by the media critically and not just *take it at face value*.

是的，我认为媒体在引导公众舆论方面发挥着重要作用。人们经常依靠电视、报纸和社交媒体等各种媒体平台来收集信息，并形成自己对不同事务的看法。不过，重要的一点是要批判性地对待媒体提供的信息，而不是只看表面现象（take something at face value）。

07 impulse buying

用法解析

impulse buying 的意思是"冲动购买",也可以说成 impulse shopping,要表达"某一次的冲动购物",可以说 an impulse buy,比如:The curtains were an impulse buy. 窗帘是一时兴起买下的。

实用语境

Do you think people should follow fashion trends? 你认为人们应该追随时尚潮流吗?

I don't think so. Although fashion can be a way for people to express their individuality, following fashion trends blindly can do more harm than good. For example, it can lead to *impulse buying* and waste of money. I think it's better for people to choose clothes that suit their personality and lifestyle, rather than buying clothes that are trendy.

我不这么认为。虽然时尚是人们表达个性的一种方式,但盲目追随时尚潮流弊大于利。例如,它可能导致冲动购物(impulse buying)和金钱浪费。我认为,人们最好选择适合自己个性和生活方式的衣服,而不是购买时髦的衣服。

08 feel comfortable in somebody's own skin

feel comfortable in somebody's own skin 是一个固定搭配，意思是"某人感到从容自信"。在表达时尚的好处时，我们可以说得体的穿着能让人感到更加从容自信。

Do you think fashion is important?
你认为时尚重要吗？

Yes, I think fashion is important because it allows people to express themselves and feel confident. For example, when people wear outfits that are trendy and visually appealing, they are more likely to *feel comfortable in their own skin*. Those who dress well also attract positive attention and compliments from others, which boosts their confidence.

是的，我认为时尚很重要，因为它能让人们表达自己以及让人们感到自信。例如，当人们穿上新潮且具有视觉吸引力的服装时，他们更容易感到从容自在（feel comfortable in their own skin）。穿着得体的人还能吸引他人的关注和赞美，从而增强自信。

09 unrealistic body standards

用法解析

该短语的意思是"不切实际的身材标准"，在阐述媒体和广告的缺点时可以用上该短语。目前不少广告里的模特往往具有完美身材，这容易树立不切实际的身材标准，让普通人感到焦虑和不自信。

实用语境

Do you think people today are more concerned about their appearance than they were in the past?
你认为今天的人们是否比过去更注重自己的外表?

Yes, I do. I think one of the main reasons for this is that people are exposed to a lot more images of perfect bodies than they used to be. Nowadays, media platforms are flooded with images of models and celebrities who often have *unrealistic body standards*. These images can create unrealistic expectations for ordinary people, leading to body image issues.

是的，我是这样认为的。我认为，造成这种情况的一个主要原因是人们接触到的完美身材照片比以前多得多。如今，媒体平台上充斥着模特和名人的照片，他们往往拥有不切实际的身材标准（unrealistic body standards）。这些照片会让普通人产生不切实际的期望，从而导致形象焦虑。

10 | something is blown out of proportion

something is blown out of proportion 的 意 思 是 "某事物被夸大了，某事物被小题大做了"，比如：The whole affair was blown out of proportion. 整个事件被渲染得太过了。该短语的主动形式是 blow something out of proportion。近 义 表 达 还 有：something is exaggerated。

用法解析

Do you think the media can influence public opinion on important matters?
你认为媒体能在重要问题上影响公众舆论吗？

实用语境

Yes, I think so. The media have the power to present information in a certain way, which can sway people's perceptions on important matters. For instance, if a particular issue is repeatedly highlighted in a sensational manner, it can *be blown out of proportion*, leading the public to perceive it as a more significant problem than it might actually be.

是的，我认为是这样。媒体有能力以某种方式呈现信息，从而左右人们对重要问题的看法。例如，如果某个问题被反复以耸人听闻的方式强调，它就会被夸大（blown out of proportion），导致公众认为它比实际情况更加严重。

11 be in the public eye

用法解析

in the public eye 的字面意思是"处于公众眼中",可引申为"受到公众关注"。在与名人有关的话题中可以用上该表达。

实用语境

What are the drawbacks of being a celebrity?
作为名人都有哪些坏处?

I think one of the drawbacks of being a celebrity is the loss of privacy. Celebrities are always *in the public eye*. They can't do anything without being scrutinized by paparazzi and their fans. Plus, the entertainment industry is highly unpredictable, which means a celebrity's popularity may not always last. In order to stay relevant, some celebrities go so far as to court publicity.

我认为,成为名人的一个弊端就是失去隐私。名人总是处在公众的视线中(in the public eye)。他们做任何事情都会受到狗仔队和粉丝的监视。此外,娱乐圈变幻莫测,这意味着名人的知名度不一定能持久。为了不被淘汰,一些名人不惜蹭热点。

12 dominate the headlines

headlines 指的是"报纸的大字标题"，可引申为"头条新闻"，dominate the headlines 可以用来指"（人物或事件）成为报纸头条新闻"。该短语也可以表达成 make/hit the headlines。

Do you think celebrities have a responsibility to be good role models?
你认为名人有责任成为好榜样吗？

Yes, I think so. Celebrities are public figures who often *dominate the headlines* and have a significant influence on people's lives. They should be aware of their impact on society, and use their influence to raise public awareness of important issues, such as poverty, pollution, and social inequality.

是的，我是这样认为的。名人是公众人物，经常占据新闻头条（dominate the headlines），能对人们的生活产生重大影响。他们应该意识到自己对社会的影响，并利用自己的影响力让公众关注到贫困、污染和社会不公等重要问题。

13 present something in a positive light

 用法解析

该短语的意思是"从积极的角度呈现某事物"，比如：Politicians often hire public relations firms to present themselves in a positive light. 政客通常会聘请公关公司来让自己以正面形象示人。该短语的反义表达是 present something in a negative light。

 实用语境

Do you think the media can bring positive changes?
你认为媒体能带来积极变化吗？

Yes. The media have the ability to promote positive social change by highlighting particular issues and *presenting them in a positive light*. For example, the media can present stories about people who are helping others, or making positive changes in their communities. This can inspire others to take action and make a difference in their own communities.

是的，媒体有能力通过突出特定议题并以积极的方式呈现这些议题来促进积极的社会变革（present them in a positive light）。例如，媒体可以报道那些帮助他人或在社区中做出积极改变的人。这可以激励其他人采取行动，为社区做出贡献。

14 somebody has a large following

该短语的意思相当于"某人拥有大批追随者"，可以用来形容名人粉丝众多。另一个可以替换的说法是 somebody has a huge fan base，比如：The Harry Potter series, written by J.K. Rowling, has a huge fan base; its magical world continues to enchant readers of all ages. 由J.K. 罗琳创作的《哈利·波特》系列拥有庞大的粉丝群，书中的魔幻世界一直吸引着各个年龄段的读者。

Do you think celebrities have a responsibility to be good role models for young people?
你认为名人有责任成为年轻人的榜样吗?

Yes, I think celebrities should be aware that they *have a large following* and that their actions and words can influence many people, especially the younger generation. So I think they have some responsibility to set a good example for their fans. For example, they should behave responsibly in their personal and professional lives, and avoid getting involved in scandals that might damage their reputation.

是的，我认为名人应该意识到他们拥有众多粉丝（have a large following）以及他们的言行会影响很多人，尤其是年轻一代。因此，我认为他们有责任为粉丝树立榜样。例如，他们应该在个人生活和职业生活中表现得负责任，以及避免卷入丑闻，以免损害自己的声誉。

15 support good causes

 用法解析

短语中的 cause 意思不是"导致",而是作为名词用时的"(为某些人所强烈支持的)原则,事业,目标",比如:They are fighting for a cause—the liberation of their people. 他们正为解放人民这一事业而战斗。短语 support good causes 即"支持公益事业",比如给慈善机构捐款、为社区做义务劳动以及参与环保活动都属于支持公益事业。

 实用语境

Do you agree that some celebrities deserve more respect and recognition than others?
你是否同意有些名人比其他人更值得尊重和认可?

Yes, I do. I think some celebrities are more talented, hardworking and genuine than others. They have achieved success and fame through their own efforts and skills, and they use their influence to *support good causes* and help others. I think they deserve more respect and recognition than those who are famous for superficial reasons or who misuse their power and fame.

是的,我是这么认为的。我认为有些名人比其他人更有才华、更勤奋、更真诚。他们通过自己的努力和技能获得成功和名声,并利用自己的影响力支持公益事业(support good causes)和帮助他人。我认为,与那些因肤浅原因成名或与那些滥用权力和名气的人相比,他们更值得尊重和认可。

16 something brings attention to

该短语的意思是"某事物让人们将注意力集中到……身上",我们可以用该表达来说明媒体或社交网络的作用。比如：The media have the power to bring attention to critical issues that might otherwise remain unnoticed, thereby playing a pivotal role in shaping public opinion. 媒体有能力让人们关注那些本来可能会被忽视的重要议题,从而在形成公众舆论方面发挥关键作用。

用法解析

What role do you think television plays in society? 你认为电视在社会中扮演了什么样的角色?

实用语境

Television plays a crucial role in society. It's a source of entertainment, education, and information. It can influence public opinion and *bring attention to* important issues such as poverty, pollution, and social injustice. However, it's essential for viewers to critically evaluate the information they receive through television.

电视在社会中发挥着至关重要的作用。它是一种获取娱乐、教育和信息的方式。它可以影响公众舆论,引发人们对贫困、污染和社会不公等重要问题的关注（bring attention to）。然而,观众必须批判性地看待电视里面的信息。

17 fit in with somebody

用法解析

该短语的意思是"与某人融洽相处，被某人接纳"，比如：
She fitted in with her new colleagues straight away.
她很快就和新同事们打成一片。fit in 也可以单独使用，
比如：I never really fitted in at school. 我在学校里从
来都不是很合群。

实用语境

Why do you think people follow fashion trends?
为什么人们追随时尚潮流？

There are several reasons why people follow fashion
trends. Firstly, fashion is a form of self-expression.
It allows individuals to showcase their personality
and individuality through their clothing choices.
Plus, following fashion trends can also be a way for
individuals to *fit in with* their peers. It gives them a
sense of belonging and acceptance within their social
circles.

人们追随时尚潮流有几个原因。首先，时尚是一
种自我表达方式。它允许人们通过服装的选择来
展示自己的个性和个人魅力。此外，追随时尚潮
流也是个人融入（fit in with）同龄人的一种方式。
这让他们在社交圈中产生归属感和被认可感。

18 personal grooming

personal grooming 的意思是"个人打扮"，比如：You should always pay attention to personal grooming. 你应随时注意个人衣着整洁。

Do you think fashion is more important to women than men?
你认为时尚对女性比对男性更重要吗?

While it's a common stereotype that women are more interested in fashion than men, I believe this perception is changing. Today, men are becoming more conscious about their appearance and the way they dress. They are investing more time and money into their wardrobe and *personal grooming*. So, I would say that fashion is equally important to both women and men.

虽然人们的刻板印象是女性比男性更关注时尚，但我相信这种看法正在发生变化。如今，男性越来越注重自己的外表和着装方式。他们在衣橱和个人打扮（personal grooming）上投入了更多的时间和金钱。因此，我认为时尚对女性和男性同样重要。

19 be appealing to somebody

用法解析

该短语的意思是"……对某人有吸引力",比如:These toys are not immediately appealing to children. 这些玩具不会让孩子们一眼就看上。另一个可供替换的说法是 something/somebody appeals to somebody,比如:The idea of working abroad really appeals to me. 去国外工作的这个想法对我很有吸引力。

实用语境

Why are some people fascinated by celebrities?
为什么有些人会对名人着迷?

I think some people are fascinated by celebrities because they often represent ideals or lifestyles that many aspire to. Celebrities are often seen as successful, glamorous, and influential, which can *be appealing to* many people. Additionally, celebrities often have talents or skills that are admired by others, such as acting, singing, or athletic abilities.

我认为有些人对名人着迷是因为名人往往代表着许多人向往的理想或生活方式。名人通常被视为成功、迷人和有影响力的人,这对很多人来说都很有吸引力(be appealing to)。此外,名人通常还拥有受人钦佩的才能或技能,如表演、唱歌或运动能力。

Part 3

科技话题

扫一扫，听录音

01 somebody can't live without something
02 do something in the comfort of our own home
03 somebody is glued to their screens
04 something has become an integral part of our lives
05 brick-and-mortar stores
06 something is just a click away
07 use technology in a more responsible way
08 a short attention span
09 escape from everyday life
10 instant gratification
11 move with the times
12 tech-savvy
13 poor posture
14 do something at your fingertips
15 screen time
16 make something readily available
17 something aids in learning
18 a digital divide
19 have instant access to something
20 compare prices
21 improve cognitive abilities

01 somebody can't live without something

用法解析

somebody can live without something 的 意 思 是 "某人可以离开某事物生活"；somebody can't live without something 即"某人的生活离不开某事物"。在科技类话题中人们经常用该表达来形容手机、互联网、社交网络以及手机游戏等被广泛使用的事物。

实用语境

What technological advancements do you think are important to our lives?
你认为哪些技术进步对我们的生活很重要?

I think smartphones are definitely one of the most important technological advancements in the 21st century. They have become an essential part of our lives and we *can't live without* them. Another one would be the internet. It has revolutionized the way we communicate and access information.

我认为智能手机绝对是 21 世纪最重要的技术进步之一。智能手机已经成为我们生活中不可或缺的一部分，我们的生活离不开它们（can't live without）。另一个是互联网。它彻底改变了我们交流和获取信息的方式。

02 do something in the comfort of our own home

该短语的意思是"在我们家中舒舒服服地做某事"，在讨论互联网的优点时经常可以用上该短语，比如 go shopping/ watch movies/ attend classes in the comfort of our own home。

用法解析

Is technology making our lives easier?
技术让我们的生活变得更加轻松吗？

实用语境

I think technology is making our lives easier in many ways. For example, we can now communicate with people all over the world with ease. We can also do things like online shopping and banking *in the comfort of our own home*. However, technology is also making our lives more complicated in some ways. For example, we are now expected to be available 24/7 because of smartphones and other devices.

我认为，技术在很多方面让我们的生活变得更轻松。例如，我们现在可以轻松地与世界各地的人们交流。我们还可以在舒适的家中（in the comfort of our own home）进行网上购物和办理银行业务等。然而，科技也在某些方面让我们的生活变得更加复杂。例如，由于智能手机和其他设备的存在，我们现在需要全天候地工作。

03 somebody is glued to their screens

用法解析

somebody is glued to their screens 是一个很形象的说法，意思相当于"某人目不转睛地盯着屏幕（就像被胶水黏住一样）"。我们可以用该短语来说明人们沉迷于手机和电脑等数码产品。

实用语境

Do you think people should limit their use of technology?
你认为人们应该限制使用技术吗？

Yes, I believe it is important for people to find a balance in their use of technology. In today's digital age, many people spend a significant amount of time *glued to their screens*, which can have adverse effects on their physical and mental well-being. It's crucial for them to be mindful of their screen time and make conscious efforts to reduce it.

是的，我认为人们在使用技术时必须有节制。在当今的数字时代，许多人花大量时间盯着屏幕（glued to their screens），这会对他们的身心健康产生不利影响。他们必须注意自己的屏幕时间，并有意识地减少使用屏幕的时间。

04 something has become an integral part of our lives

该表达的意思是"某事物已经成为我们生活中不可或缺的一部分",我们可以用该说法来形容科技产品在生活中的重要性。比如我们可以说 the internet/smartphones/computers/social media have (has) become an integral part of our lives。

用法解析

Do you think people are getting addicted to their phones?
你觉得人们对手机越来越上瘾吗?

实用语境

Yes, I think so. Smartphones have *become such an integral part of our lives* that we can't imagine living without them. People are constantly checking their phones for messages, notifications, and updates. It's like they can't put them down.

是的,我是这样认为的。智能手机已经成为我们生活中不可或缺的一部分(become an integral part of our lives),以至于我们无法想象没有手机的生活。人们总是不停地查看手机上的信息、通知和更新。就好像他们无法放下手机。

05 brick-and-mortar stores

用法解析

brick-and-mortar stores 的意思是"实体店，线下店"，在与电商相关的话题中会经常出现这一说法，它也可以说成 bricks-and-mortar stores。与它对应的则是 online stores，即"线上店"。

实用语境

Do you think online shopping will replace in-store shopping in the future?
你认为网络购物会在未来替代线下购物吗？

I don't think so. Although online shopping is growing in popularity, there are still many people who prefer to shop in *brick-and-mortar stores*. For example, some people like to try on clothes before buying them, which is only possible in traditional stores. Also, some people enjoy the experience of going to a physical store and browsing through products. So I think brick-and-mortar stores will continue to exist alongside online shopping.

我不这么认为。虽然线上购物越来越受欢迎，但仍有很多人喜欢到实体店购物（brick-and-mortar stores）。例如，有些人喜欢在买衣服前试穿，这只有在线下商店才有可能。此外，有些人喜欢逛实体店的那种感觉。因此，我认为实体店将继续与线上购物并存。

06 something is just a click away

click 的意思是"鼠标的点击"。Something is just a click away 意思是"某事物只要点点鼠标就可以获得"。我们可以用该表述来说明互联网的便利性。

用法解析

Has technology changed the way we get information?
技术改变了我们获取信息的方式吗？

实用语境

Yes, I think technology has revolutionized the way we get information. In the past, acquiring knowledge required extensive research through books and encyclopedias. However, with the rise of the internet, information is *just a click away*. Through search engines and online platforms, we have instant access to information on any topic we want.

是的，我认为技术彻底改变了我们获取信息的方式。过去，获取知识需要通过书籍或百科全书。然而，随着互联网的兴起，只需点击一下鼠标（just a click away），就能获得信息。通过搜索引擎和在线平台，我们可以随时获取我们想要的任何主题的信息。

07 use technology in a more responsible way

用法解析

responsible 除了可以理解为"有责任感的",还有一个重要义项为"明智的,可靠的",此时它的意思类似于 sensible。比如:Let's stay calm and try to behave like responsible adults. 让我们冷静下来,行事尽量拿出成年人应有的明辨是非的能力。

use technology in a more responsible way 的意思是"明智地使用科技产品",即不过度使用手机、电脑等产品。近义表达还有 use technology responsibly。

实用语境

What are some of the negative effects of technology on society?

技术对社会造成了哪些负面影响?

I think one of the negative effects of technology is that people are becoming more isolated and less social. For example, people are spending more time on their phones and computers and less time interacting with others in person. To avoid these problems, we should *use technology in a more responsible way*.

我认为,科技的负面影响之一是人们变得更加孤立,社交越来越少。例如,人们花在手机和电脑上的时间越来越多,而与人交流的时间却越来越少。为了避免这些问题,我们应该以更加负责任的方式使用科技产品(use technology in a more responsible way)。

08 a short attention span

a short attention span 的意思是"注意力时间不足"，比如：Children often have a short attention span. 小孩子的注意力持续时间往往都很短。在讨论手机和网络带来的负面影响时经常会出现这个说法。

用法解析

How do you think smartphones have affected people's daily lives?
你认为智能手机对人们的日常生活有何影响？

实用语境

I think smartphones enable people to access vast amounts of information at their fingertips. This has made tasks such as information gathering and communication much more convenient and efficient. However, they also bring some challenges. For instance, with the rise of social media and instant messaging apps, people tend to have *a short attention span*. They find it difficult to concentrate on a single task for an extended period of time.

我认为，智能手机使人们能够触手可及地获取大量信息。这使得信息收集和交流等工作变得更加方便和高效。然而，智能手机也带来了一些挑战。例如，随着社交媒体和即时通信应用程序的兴起，人们的注意力往往不够集中（a short attention span）。他们发现很难长时间专注于一项任务。

09　escape from everyday life

该短语的意思是"从日常生活中解脱出来"，我们可以用它来描述电影、游戏、阅读以及旅行等活动的好处，比如：Watching movies can be a good way to escape from everyday life, transporting you to different worlds and adventures. 看电影是从日常生活中解脱出来的好方法，它能把你带到不同的世界和冒险中去。

Why do some people prefer watching a film in the cinema rather than at home?
为什么有些人喜欢在电影院而不是在家看电影？

There are several reasons why some people prefer watching a film in the cinema rather than at home. Firstly, the cinema provides a larger screen and better sound quality, which can enhance the viewing experience. Secondly, going to the cinema can be a social activity, where people can enjoy the film with their friends or family. Lastly, watching a film in the cinema can be a way to *escape from everyday life* and immerse oneself in a different world for a few hours.

有些人喜欢在电影院而不是在家里看电影，这有几个原因。首先，电影院的银幕更大，音质更好，可以提升观影体验。其次，去电影院可以是一种社交活动，人们可以与朋友或家人一起欣赏电影。最后，在电影院看电影可以让人从日常生活中解脱出来（escape from everyday life），连续几个小时沉浸在不同的世界中。

10 instant gratification

instant gratification 的意思是"即时满足"，这是科技话题中的一个高频表达。比如互联网带来了"即时满足"的刺激。网上各种娱乐内容随手可得，这虽然带来了便利性，但也让人们变得更加没有耐心。即时满足的对立面则是 delayed gratification（延迟满足）。

What are some of the negative effects of modern technology?
现代科技都有哪些负面影响？

I think one downside of modern technology is that people can become too reliant on their digital devices and lose touch with the real world. Another problem is that modern technology has led to *instant gratification*. People expect everything to be available at their fingertips and have become impatient when they have to wait for anything.

我认为，现代技术的一个弊端是人们会变得过于依赖数字设备，从而与现实世界脱节。另一个问题是现代技术导致了即时满足感（instant gratification）。人们希望一切都能唾手可得。当他们需要等待时就会变得不耐烦。

11 | move with the times

用法解析

move with the times 的意思即"与时俱进"，同义表达还有 change with the times, keep up with the times。注意 times 是复数形式。

 实用语境

Do you think people should embrace new technology? 你认为人们应该拥抱新技术吗？

Yes, I think it's important to *move with the times* and embrace new technology. Technology is constantly evolving and improving, and it's important to keep up with these changes if you want to stay competitive in today's world. By adopting new technology, you can improve your productivity, efficiency, and overall quality of life.

是的，我认为与时俱进（move with the times）、拥抱新技术非常重要。技术在不断发展和改进，要想在当今世界保持竞争力，就必须跟上这些变化。通过采用新技术，你可以提高生产力、效率和整体生活质量。

12 tech-savvy

savvy 作形容词时的意思是"精明的，有见识的"，例如：savvy consumers 精明的消费者。tech-savvy 的意思是"精通科技产品的"，比如英文媒体经常将年轻一代称为 tech-savvy millennials（精通科技产品的千禧一代）。

Do you think it is important to use digital products well?
你认为用好数码产品重要吗？

Absolutely, being *tech-savvy* is becoming increasingly essential in today's digital age. As technology permeates into every aspect of our lives, having a good understanding of digital products and their functionalities helps people improve their productivity and stay informed. For example, tech-savvy workers can make good use of digital tools to accomplish tasks in less time.

当然，在当今的数字时代，精通科技产品（tech-savvy）变得越来越重要。随着技术渗透到我们生活的方方面面，充分了解数码产品及其功能有助于提高人们的工作效率和保持信息畅通。例如，精通科技产品的员工可以很好地利用数字工具，在更短的时间内完成任务。

13 | poor posture

用法解析

posture 的意思是"姿态，姿势"，poor posture 即我们常说的"不良姿势"。要表达"某人仪态优美"，可以说：Somebody has good posture。使用电子设备的一个常见缺点就是它会导致不良姿势。

实用语境

Do you think the use of smartphones will bring negative effects?
你认为使用智能手机会带来负面影响吗？

Yes, overuse of smartphones can lead to health issues like eye strain and *poor posture*. It can also lead to addiction, affecting our social interactions and productivity. Moreover, excessive use of smartphones can invade our privacy and make us vulnerable to cyber threats.

是的，过度使用智能手机会导致眼睛疲劳和姿势不良（poor posture）等健康问题。它还可能导致成瘾，影响我们的社交互动和工作效率。此外，过度使用智能手机还会侵犯我们的隐私，使我们容易受到网络攻击。

14 do something at your fingertips

用法解析

at your fingertips 的字面意思是"近在手边"，引申为"很容易得到，随时可供使用"，我们可以用 do something at your fingertips 来表示"做某事很容易"。在涉及科技相关的话题时经常可以用上该表达。比如：With a smartphone in your pocket, you have the world's knowledge at your fingertips. 只要口袋中有部智能手机，全世界的知识随时都可获得。

How have smartphones changed our lives?
智能手机如何改变我们的生活？

实用语境

Smartphones have revolutionized our lives in many ways. They have become an integral part of our daily routine. We use them for communication, entertainment, information, and even for work. They have made it easier to stay connected with people around the world, access information *at our fingertips*, and manage our tasks efficiently.

智能手机在许多方面都彻底改变了我们的生活。它们已成为我们日常生活中不可或缺的一部分。我们用它来交流、娱乐、获取信息，甚至工作。智能手机让我们更容易与世界各地的人们保持联系，随时随地（at our fingertips）获取信息，并高效地管理我们的任务。

15 screen time

用法解析

screen time 是指人们花在手机和电脑等电子产品上面的时间，这是一个科技类话题中的万能表达。要限制科技对人们的影响，一个方法是限制人们的屏幕时间。

实用语境

What measures do you think can be taken to mitigate the negative impacts of smartphones?
你认为可以采取哪些措施来减轻智能手机的负面影响？

There are several strategies that can be employed to manage smartphone usage effectively. On an individual level, people can limit their *screen time* and make conscious efforts to engage in offline activities. On a societal level, there could be more public awareness campaigns about the potential harms of excessive smartphone use. Schools could incorporate digital literacy into their curriculum, teaching students about responsible smartphone use.

有几种策略可以有效管理智能手机的使用。就个人而言，人们可以限制他们的屏幕时间（screen time），并有意识地参与线下活动。在社会层面，可以开展更多的公众宣传活动，让人们认识到过度使用智能手机的潜在危害。学校可以将数字扫盲纳入课程，教导学生负责任地使用智能手机。

16 make something readily available

用法解析

该短语的意思是"让某事物变得触手可及"，我们可以用该表达来说明互联网让信息变得触手可及，网购让各种商品和服务变得触手可及等，比如：E-commerce websites make a wide range of products readily available to consumers, transforming the shopping experience. 电子商务网站为消费者提供了种类繁多的产品，改变了购物体验。

How has technology impacted language learning? 技术如何影响语言学习？

实用语境

Technology has indeed revolutionized the way we learn languages. With the advent of language learning apps, learners can now access high-quality language instruction at their fingertips. Online platforms also offer video calling features that allow learners to practice speaking with native speakers from around the world. Furthermore, technology has *made* resources like dictionaries and translators *readily available*, making it easier for learners to overcome challenges they may face during the learning process.

技术的确彻底改变了我们学习语言的方式。随着语言学习应用软件的出现，学习者现在可以随时随地获得高质量的语言教学指导。在线平台还提供视频通话功能，学习者可以与世界各地的母语人士练习口语。此外，技术还让词典和翻译等资源变得唾手可得（make something readily available），使学习者更容易克服学习过程中可能面临的挑战。

17 something aids in learning

用法解析

Something aids in something 的意思是"某事物有助于……"，比如：The new test should aid in the early detection of the disease. 新的化验应该有助于早早检查出这种疾病。Something aids in learning 即表示"某事物有助于学习"，我们可以用该表述来说明电子游戏、短视频以及电视等科技产品对学习的助益。

实用语境

What impact do you think video games have on children?
你认为电子游戏会对儿童产生什么影响？

Video games can have both positive and negative impacts on children. On the positive side, they can help develop problem-solving and strategic thinking skills. Some educational games can also *aid in learning*. However, excessive gaming can lead to addiction and social isolation. It's important for parents to monitor their children's gaming habits and ensure they are balanced with other activities.

电子游戏对儿童既有积极影响，也有消极影响。积极的一面是电子游戏有助于培养儿童解决问题和战略思维的能力。一些益智游戏也有助于学习（aid in learning）。但是，过度游戏会导致成瘾和社交隔离。家长必须监督孩子的游戏习惯，并确保游戏与其他活动保持平衡。

18 a digital divide

a digital divide 是近年来比较流行的一个词，意思是"数字鸿沟"，指那些能用上电脑和互联网的人与那些无法用上这些科技产品的人之间的差距。如何减少"数字鸿沟"也是一个热门议题。比如：A digital divide is evident in rural areas where the infrastructure for high-speed internet is often lacking, thus limiting opportunities for education and business. 农村地区的数字鸿沟非常明显，那里往往缺乏高速互联网基础设施，从而限制了教育和商业。

用法解析

Do you see any potential downsides to the increased use of technology in education?
你认为技术在教育中的大量使用有什么潜在的弊端吗？

实用语境

There are some concerns. Overreliance on technology might lead to a lack of personal interaction among students and teachers. It could also create *a digital divide*, where some students have better access to technology than others, potentially exacerbating educational inequalities.

确实存在一些担忧。过度依赖技术可能会导致师生之间缺乏个人互动。它还可能造成数字鸿沟（a digital divide），即一些学生比其他学生更容易获得技术，从而可能加剧教育不平等。

19 have instant access to something

用法解析

该短语的意思是"能够立即获取某事物"，该表达经常用于讨论互联网的便利性，比如人们可以在网上快速获取知识、音乐和电影等各种信息。

实用语境

How has technology changed the way people communicate in your country?
在你们国家，技术如何改变了人们的交流方式？

Technology has revolutionized communication in my country. People now *have instant access to* various tools like social media, emails, and instant messaging apps. This has made communication faster and more efficient. People can now connect with others across the globe in real time, which was not possible before. It has also made information sharing much easier and quicker.

在我们国家，技术彻底改变了人们的交流方式。人们现在可以方便地使用（have instant access to）社交媒体、电子邮件和即时通信应用程序等各种工具。这使得交流更加快捷高效。人们现在可以与全球各地的其他人实时联系，这在以前是不可能的。这也使信息共享变得更加方便快捷。

20 compare prices

compare prices 即我们常说的"比价"，在电商购物话题中，我们经常会用到这个表达，比如可以说：Online shopping enables consumers to compare prices from different retailers, making it easier for them to find the best deal for their desired products. 网上购物使消费者能够比较不同商家的价格，从而更容易以满意的价格买到心仪的产品。

用法解析

Can you elaborate on the advantages of online shopping?
你能详细介绍一下网上购物的优势吗？

实用语境

Of course. The primary advantage of online shopping is convenience. It eliminates the need to travel to a physical store, which can save a lot of time and energy. Additionally, online stores often have a wider variety of products than physical stores, and it's easier to *compare prices* and read reviews on the internet.

当然可以。网上购物的首要优势是方便。它省去了前往实体店的麻烦，可以节省大量的时间和精力。此外，网店的产品种类通常比实体店更丰富，而且在网上比较商品价格（compare prices）和阅读评论也更容易。

21 improve cognitive abilities

 用法解析

该短语的意思是"提升认知能力"，这一表达在教育类和科技类话题中有很广泛的应用。在描述玩具、电子游戏、阅读以及学习外语的好处时都可以用上该短语。比如：Learning a new language at any age can significantly improve cognitive abilities, fostering problem-solving skills and enhancing multitasking capabilities. 在任何年龄段学习一门新的语言，都能显著提高认知能力，培养解决问题的技能以及增强多任务处理能力。

 实用语境

Can you elaborate on the positive aspects of video games for young people?
你能详细谈谈电子游戏对青少年的积极意义吗？

Of course. Video games can enhance problem-solving skills and strategic thinking. For example, many games require players to make quick decisions and adapt to changing situations. They can also be a source of social interaction when played with friends online. Moreover, some games can be educational and help *improve cognitive abilities*.

当然可以。电子游戏可以提高解决问题的能力和战略思维。例如，许多游戏要求玩家迅速做出决定并适应不断变化的情况。与朋友在线玩游戏时，电子游戏还是一种社交互动的形式。此外，有些游戏还具有教育意义，有助于提高认知能力（improve cognitive abilities）。

Part 4

健康话题

扫一扫，听录音

01 stay active

02 be rich in something

03 ... is a good way to enjoy the outdoors

04 take a break from ...

05 lead a sedentary lifestyle

06 do a good workout

07 keep somebody's figure

08 have an excessive consumption of processed foods and sugary drinks

09 something reduces the risk of chronic diseases

10 incorporate physical activities into somebody's daily routine

11 improve somebody's hand-eye coordination

12 make informed food choices

13 excessive exposure to screens

14 be high in salt and sugar

15 cook your own meals

16 improve somebody's motor skills

17 plant-based diets

01 stay active

用法解析

这是一个很简单的表达，但口语中能主动使用的同学并不多。stay active 的意思相当于"经常运动的"，它在运动和健康话题中有广泛的应用。与之意思相近的说法是 lead an active lifestyle 或者 live an active life。

实用语境

Do you think it's important to spend time outdoors?
你认为户外活动重要吗？

Yes, I think it's important to spend time outdoors because it's a great way to relax and get away from the pressures of work. It's also a good way to *stay active* and healthy. You can make the most of your time outdoors by doing outdoor activities like going for a walk in the park, or playing soccer or basketball with your friends.

是的，我认为户外活动很重要，因为这是放松身心、摆脱工作压力的好方法。这也是保持活跃（stay active）和健康的好方法。你可以通过户外活动充分利用户外时间，比如去公园散步，或与朋友一起踢足球或打篮球。

02 be rich in something

... is rich in something 的意思是 "……富含某事物"，在讨论食物的营养成分时我们就可以用上该说法，比如要表达 "橙子富含维生素 C"，可以说：Oranges are rich in vitamin C. 该表达也可以表述为：... is high in something.

用法解析

What kinds of foods do you think are healthy?
哪种食物你认为是健康食物？

实用语境

I believe that foods that are *rich in* essential nutrients are healthy. For instance, fruits and vegetables are an integral part of a healthy diet as they are rich in vitamins, minerals, and dietary fiber. Whole grains are also important as they provide complex carbohydrates and fiber.

我觉得富含（rich in）基本营养素的食物是健康食品。例如，水果和蔬菜是健康饮食的一个组成部分，因为它们富含维生素、矿物质和膳食纤维。全谷物也很重要，因为它们提供复杂的碳水化合物和纤维。

03 ... is a good way to enjoy the outdoors

用法解析

the outdoors 的意思是"户外环境、自然环境",注意不要记成 the outdoor。在描述露营、登山、野餐、骑行等户外活动带来的好处时我们可以用上该表达。比如我们可以说:Camping/Hiking/Picnicking/Cycling is a good way to enjoy the outdoors.

实用语境

How do you think people can make the most of their free time outdoors?
你认为人们应该如何充分利用空闲时间进行户外活动?

I believe engaging in outdoor sports and recreational activities is *a good way to enjoy the outdoors*. For example, playing football in the park with friends not only allows you to stay active but also provides an opportunity to enjoy the natural surroundings and fresh air.

我认为参加户外运动和娱乐活动是享受户外活动的好方法(a good way to enjoy the outdoors)。例如,与朋友一起在公园踢足球,不仅可以让你保持活跃,还能享受自然环境和新鲜空气。

04 take a break from …

break 在这里的意思是"休息，假期"，比如 have a winter break 的意思是"休寒假"。要表达"休假，暂停工作"，可以说 take a break from work。

用法解析

What can people do to reduce stress?
人们可以做哪些事情来减少压力？

实用语境

There are many things that people can do to manage their stress levels. For example, they can engage in stress-relieving activities such as yoga or meditation. They can also *take a break from* work and spend time with friends and family. Finally, they can seek professional help if their stress levels become too high.

人们可以做很多事情来减少压力。例如，他们可以做一些能够减轻压力的活动，如瑜伽或冥想。他们也可以暂停一下工作（take a break from work），花时间与朋友和家人在一起。最后，如果他们的压力实在太大，他们可以寻求专业人士的帮助。

05 lead a sedentary lifestyle

用法解析

sedentary 的意思是"久坐不动的"，lead a sedentary lifestyle 即"倾向于久坐的生活方式"，该短语也可以表达为 live a sedentary lifestyle。要描述一个需要久坐的工作，可以说 a sedentary job。

实用语境

Do you think people should be encouraged to do more exercise?
你认为应该鼓励人们多做运动吗？

Definitely. Nowadays, people *lead a sedentary lifestyle* and spend most of their time sitting in front of computers or watching TV. This can lead to many health problems such as obesity and heart disease. Exercise is a great way to stay healthy and prevent these problems.

当然。如今，人们过着久坐不动的生活（lead a sedentary lifestyle），他们大部分时间都坐在电脑前或看电视。这可能会导致许多健康问题，如肥胖和心脏疾病。锻炼是保持健康和预防这些问题的一个好方法。

06 do a good workout

workout 的意思是"体育锻炼，运动"，注意 workout 是可数名词，要表达"持续 20 分钟的有氧运动"，可以说 a 20-minute aerobic workout。短语 do a good workout 的意思相当于"进行适当的运动"。

用法解析

How do you stay fit and healthy?
你如何保持健康？

实用语境

Well, I believe in maintaining an active lifestyle to stay healthy. One of the ways I do that is by engaging in regular physical exercise. I enjoy going to the gym and *doing a good workout* at least three times a week. It helps me burn calories and increase metabolism.

我觉得要通过经常运动来保持健康。我的一个方法是定期参加体育锻炼。我喜欢去健身房，每周至少进行三次适当的锻炼（do a good workout）。这有助于我燃烧热量，提高新陈代谢。

07 keep somebody's figure

 用法解析

figure 在这里的含义是"身材，体形"，要表达"她身材很好"，可以说：She has a good figure. 短语 keep somebody's figure 即表示"保持某人的身材"。在说明健康饮食和运动的好处时我们可以用上该短语。

 实用语境

What are some effective ways for people to manage their weight?
有哪些可以控制体重的有效方法？

I think there are two ways individuals can *keep their figure.* Firstly, engaging in regular exercise such as jogging, cycling can help burn calories and maintain a healthy weight. Secondly, it pays to avoid food additives and eat only wholefoods like fruits, vegetables, and whole grains.

我认为有两种方法可以让人们保持身材（keep their figure）。第一，进行像慢跑、骑自行车这样的规律运动可以帮助燃烧热量并保持健康体重。第二，要避免食品添加剂，只吃水果、蔬菜和全谷物等天然食品。

08 have an excessive consumption of processed foods and sugary drinks

consumption 在这里的意思是"食用,饮用",要表达"某物不合适人类食用",可以说 Something is unfit for human consumption。processed foods 的意思是"加工食品",比如罐头、黄油、火腿这些都属于加工食品。sugary drinks 意思则是"含糖饮料"。该短语的含义是"过度食用加工食品以及含糖饮料",我们在讨论健康食品时可以用上该表达。

Do you think people are more health-conscious now than they were in the past?
你认为人们比以前更加重视健康吗?

I think today people care more about their health than in the past. However, there is still room for improvement. For example, many people still *have an excessive consumption of processed foods and sugary drinks*, which can lead to obesity and other health problems.

我认为今天人们比过去更关心自己的健康。然而,这仍有进步的空间。例如,许多人仍然过度食用加工食品和含糖饮料(have an excessive consumption of processed foods and sugary drinks),这可能导致肥胖和其他健康问题。

09 something reduces the risk of chronic diseases

用法解析

该短语的意思是"某事物能减少慢性疾病的风险"。举个例子，运动、充足睡眠以及健康饮食都能够减少慢性疾病的风险。英语中常见的慢性疾病有糖尿病（ diabetes /ˌdaɪəˈbɪtɪs/ ）、心脏病、高血压（ hypertension ）、关节炎（ arthritis /ɑːˈθraɪtəs/ ）等。

实用语境

Do you think regular exercise is important?
你认为定期锻炼重要吗？

Yes, regular exercise is extremely important because it can improve cardiovascular health, increase muscle strength, and enhance flexibility. It also aids in weight management and *reduces the risk of chronic diseases* such as hypertension and diabetes. Additionally, exercise has mental health benefits by reducing stress and improving mood.

是的，定期锻炼非常重要，因为它可以改善心血管健康、增强肌肉力量和灵活性。它还有助于控制体重，降低罹患高血压和糖尿病等慢性疾病的风险（ reduce the risk of chronic diseases ）。此外，运动还能减轻压力和改善情绪，对心理健康有益。

10 incorporate physical activities into somebody's daily routine

incorporate ... into something 的意思是"将……加入某事物当中",比如:We have incorporated all the latest safety features into the design. 我们在设计中纳入了所有最新的安全装置。短语 incorporate physical activities into somebody's daily routine 意思即"将运动纳入某人的日程表中"。在与运动相关的话题中,我们可以用上该表达。

What can be done to encourage people to exercise more?

如何鼓励人们加强锻炼?

Governments and communities can play a significant role here. They can provide safe and affordable sports facilities, organize community fitness events, and promote the benefits of regular exercise through various media channels. Plus, individuals should be encouraged to set realistic goals, find activities they enjoy, and try to *incorporate physical activities into their daily routine*.

政府和社区可以在这方面发挥重要作用。它们可以提供安全和容易负担的体育设施,组织社区健身活动,并通过各种媒体渠道宣传经常锻炼的好处。此外,还应该鼓励个人制订切实可行的目标,找到自己喜欢的活动,并努力将体育活动纳入日常生活(incorporate physical activities into somebody's daily routine)。

11 improve somebody's hand-eye coordination

 用法解析

hand-eye coordination 即我们常说的 "手眼协调"，它是指眼睛和手的精细配合能力。短语 improve somebody's hand-eye coordination 也是运动话题中的 "万能表达"，只要提及运动带来的好处时，我们都可以用上该表达。

 实用语境

What are some of the benefits of playing sports?
运动都有哪些好处？

Well, I think playing sports can help people *improve their hand-eye coordination* and develop their motor skills. It can also be a good way for them to make friends and build social skills like teamwork skills and leadership skills.

我认为运动可以帮助人们提高手眼协调能力（improve somebody's hand-eye coordination）以及发展他们的运动技能。运动也能够帮助他们交朋友和培养社会技能，如团队合作技能和领导技能。

12 make informed food choices

an informed choice 是一个固定说法，意思是"明智的选择，可靠的选择"。make informed food choices 即表示"在饮食上做出明智的选择"，该短语在口语中一般用于表达选择吃健康食品，以及避免那些深度加工的食物的含义。

 用法解析

Do you think people should be more aware of what they eat?
你认为人们应该更加注意自己的饮食吗？

 实用语境

Absolutely. I believe that it's important for people to *make informed food choices*. For instance, they should be aware of the nutritional value of the food they eat and how it affects their health. They should also know how to read food labels and understand what they mean. This way, they can make better decisions about what they eat.

是的，我认为人们应该在饮食上做出明智的选择（make informed food choices），这一点是很重要的。例如，他们应该知道他们所吃的食物的营养价值，以及该食物如何影响他们的健康。他们还应该知道如何阅读食品标签并理解其含义。这样，他们可以对自己的饮食选择做出更好的决定。

13 excessive exposure to screens

用法解析

exposure 这个词在口语中很好用，它的意思是"接触，经受"。比如"长时间晒太阳"可以表述为 prolonged exposure to the sun。 短 语 excessive exposure to screens 表示"在屏幕前时间太久"，这是一种需要避免的生活方式。其同义表达为：take regular screen breaks。

实用语境

What are some effective ways for people to stay healthy?
有哪些有效保持健康的方法?

Firstly, people can eat a balanced diet, exercise regularly, and get enough sleep. Secondly, they should avoid smoking and drinking alcohol in excess. Another important thing is to avoid *excessive exposure to screens*, as this can lead to eye strain and other health problems.

首先，人们可以保持饮食均衡，定期锻炼，并获得足够的睡眠。其次，他们应该避免吸烟和过量饮酒。另一件重要的事情是避免在屏幕前太久（avoid excessive exposure to screens），因为这可能导致眼睛疲劳和其他健康问题。

14 be high in salt and sugar

用法解析

be high in something 意为"某事物的含量过高"，be high in salt and sugar 即"盐和糖的含量过高"。一般来说，含盐和糖过多的食品对人的健康都有害，因此人们在形容垃圾食品时可以用上该表达。

实用语境

What do you think are some common health problems people face today?
你认为当今人们面临的常见健康问题有哪些？

One of the most common health problems is obesity, which is often caused by eating too much food that is *high in salt and sugar*, such as fast food and processed snacks. Another common problem is stress. Many people lead very busy lives and don't take enough time to unwind, which can lead to physical and mental health issues.

最常见的一种健康问题是肥胖，这通常是由于吃了太多高盐和高糖的食物（high in salt and sugar）导致的，如快餐和深加工零食。另一个常见的问题是压力过大。许多人的生活非常忙碌，没有足够的时间来放松，这可能导致身心健康问题。

15 cook your own meals

用法解析

该短语的意思为"自己做饭"，与在外面吃饭（eat out）相比，自己做饭能带来很多好处，是值得提倡的健康生活习惯。这一短语在健康饮食话题中经常出现。该短语也可以说成 cook at home。

实用语境

Do you think people are more health-conscious nowadays?
你认为现在的人们会更加重视健康吗？

Yes, I think today people are more aware of the importance of a healthy lifestyle and are taking steps to improve their health. For example, many people are now choosing to *cook their own meals* instead of eating out. This gives them more control over the ingredients, which can help them maintain a healthy weight.

是的，我认为今天人们更加意识到健康生活方式的重要性，并正在采取措施改善他们的健康。例如，许多人现在选择自己做饭（cook their own meals）而不是在外面吃饭。这让他们对食材有更多的控制，从而帮助他们保持健康的体重。

16 improve somebody's motor skills

motor skills 的意思是"运动技能"，它是指有效运用骨骼肌的技能。在关于体育锻炼好处的讨论中，一个常见的说法就是体育锻炼能够提升人的运动技能（特别是提升儿童的运动技能）。

用法解析

How do you think playing sports can benefit children?
你认为参加体育运动对儿童有什么好处？

实用语境

Playing sports helps *improve children's motor skills* and coordination. When children actively participate in sports, they engage in various movements that require coordination between their hands, feet, and body. This constant practice helps them develop and refine their motor skills, which can have long-term positive effects on their overall physical abilities.

参加体育运动有助于提高儿童的运动技能（improve somebody's motor skills）和协调能力。当儿童积极参加体育活动时，他们要进行各种需要手、脚和身体之间协调的运动。这种持续练习能帮助他们发展和完善他们的运动技能，这对他们的整体运动能力有长期的积极影响。

17 plant-based diets

用法解析

plant-based diets是近年来西方比较流行的一个说法，意思是"植物性饮食"，即以摄取蔬菜和水果这些植物性食材为主的饮食法。很多人认为这种饮食方式更有利于健康，因为它包含更少的脂肪、盐和糖。

实用语境

Why do some people choose to follow a vegetarian diet?

为什么有些人会选择素食?

There could be several reasons for this choice. Some people follow a vegetarian diet due to religious beliefs. Others might choose this lifestyle for health reasons as *plant-based diets* are often lower in fat and higher in fiber. Additionally, some people choose vegetarianism out of concern for animal welfare or environmental sustainability.

这一选择背后可能有几个原因。有些人出于宗教信仰而选择素食。其他人可能出于健康原因选择这种生活方式，因为植物性饮食（plant-based diets）通常脂肪含量较低，纤维含量较高。此外，有些人选择素食是出于对动物福利或环境可持续性的关注。

扫一扫，听录音

教育话题

Part 5

01 want the best for somebody
02 hang out with the wrong crowd
03 impart knowledge
04 a love of learning
05 fly the nest
06 academic pursuits
07 well-rounded students
08 spend quality time with
09 be free from distractions
10 learn at your own pace
11 age-appropriate
12 positive reinforcement
13 distract somebody from their studies
14 rote memorization
15 delve deep into a field of somebody's interest
16 instill good values in somebody
17 set a positive example for somebody
18 culture shock
19 something is tailored specifically to somebody
20 be conducive to learning
21 something is a form of escapism

01 want the best for somebody

用法解析

该短语的意思是"希望给某人提供最好的东西，希望给某人最好的条件"。在家庭和学校教育话题中，我们可以用该短语来说明家长和老师对孩子的关爱，比如：Parents all want the best for their children. 家长都想给孩子提供最好的条件。

实用语境

What parents are good parents?
什么样的父母是好的父母？

I believe that good parents should always *want the best for* their children and prioritize their well-being above everything else. Additionally, good parents should be able to provide guidance and support to their children, while also giving them the freedom to explore and learn from their own experiences.

我认为好的父母应该总是希望给自己的孩子提供最好的东西（want the best for），并将孩子的福祉置于一切之上。此外，一个好的父母应该能够为他们的孩子提供指导和支持，同时也给孩子自由，让他们自己去探索和学习。

02 hang out with the wrong crowd

the wrong crowd 的意思是"不良群体"，hang out with the wrong crowd 即"与不良群体混在一起"。在家庭教育中，家长的责任之一就是防止小孩与不良群体交往，以免被他们影响。

用法解析

What can parents do to help their children choose friends?
家长应该怎样帮助孩子选择朋友?

实用语境

I think parents can encourage their children to join clubs or groups that they are interested in. They can also talk to their children about what makes a good friend and what to look for in a friend. Finally, parents can monitor their children's social media use and keep an eye on who they are making friend with to make sure that their children do not *hang out with the wrong crowd*.

我认为父母可以鼓励他们的孩子加入他们感兴趣的俱乐部或团体。他们还可以与孩子讨论什么样的朋友才是好朋友，以及朋友应该拥有哪些素质。最后，父母可以监督孩子的社交媒体使用情况，并留意他们与谁交朋友，以确保他们的孩子不跟不良人群来往（hang out with the wrong crowd）。

03 impart knowledge

用法解析

impart knowledge 的意思是"传授知识"，这是一个教育话题中的高频表达，在谈及教师以及书籍的作用时可以用上它。该短语的一个常见搭配是 impart knowledge to somebody，比如：He has clever ways of imparting knowledge to his students. 他以巧妙的方式向学生传授知识。

实用语境

Do you think teachers are important in today's world? 你认为教师在当今世界重要吗？

Absolutely. Teachers play a vital role in shaping the future of their students. They not only *impart knowledge* but also help students develop critical thinking skills and creativity. By nurturing young minds, teachers can help students become well-rounded individuals who are capable of making a positive impact on society.

当然。教师在塑造学生的未来方面发挥着重要作用。他们不仅传授知识（impart knowledge），还帮助学生开发批判性思维能力和创造力。通过培养年轻人，教师可以帮助学生成为全面发展的人，并对社会产生积极影响。

04 a love of learning

该短语的意思是"对知识的热爱"，它也可以说成 a love for learning。在学习话题中，另一个经常出现的说法是 a love of reading，即"对阅读的热爱"，比如"帮助小孩培养对阅读的兴趣"可以说 help children develop a love of reading。

How can parents contribute to their children's education?
父母如何为子女的教育做出贡献？

There are many things parents can do to actively support their children's education. For example, they can foster *a love of learning* by creating a supportive environment at home. This can be done by encouraging their children to explore different subjects and providing them with good educational resources.

父母可以做很多事情来积极支持子女的教育。例如，他们可以通过在家里创造一个有利的环境来培养孩子对学习的热爱（foster a love of learning）。这可以通过鼓励孩子探索不同的科目并为他们提供良好的教育资源来实现。

05 fly the nest

 用法解析

fly the nest 的字面意思是"飞离鸟巢",它引申为"搬出父母家,离家独立",这是一个家庭教育类话题中经常会用到的表达。它也可以写成 leave the nest。

 实用语境

What are some of the challenges that young people face when they leave home?

年轻人离家时会面临哪些挑战?

I think one of the biggest challenges is loneliness. When young people *fly the nest*, they may find it hard to adjust to a new environment where they are away their family and friends. Another challenge is financial management. They need to learn how to budget their money and pay their bills on time.

我认为最大的挑战之一是孤独感。当年轻人离家独立(fly the nest)时,他们可能会发现很难适应一个远离家人和朋友的新环境。另一个挑战是财务管理。他们需要学习如何安排自己的开支,并按时支付账单。

06 academic pursuits

pursuit 这个词除了可以表示"追求"之外，还可以表示"活动"（an activity that you enjoy），academic pursuits 即"学术活动"。其他搭配还有 sporting pursuits（体育活动），leisure pursuits（娱乐活动），artistic pursuits（艺术活动），比如：She has time now to follow her various artistic pursuits. 她现在有时间从事各种艺术活动了。

Do you think that studies should be the only focus of university students?
你认为大学生应该只关注学业吗？

I don't think so. While *academic pursuits* are important, university students should also focus on other aspects of their lives such as extracurricular activities and socializing. These activities can help students develop important life skills and broaden their outlook.

我不这么认为。虽然学术活动很重要（academic pursuits），但大学生也应该关注他们生活的其他方面，如课外活动和社交。这些活动可以帮助学生培养重要的生活技能，并拓宽他们的视野。

07 well-rounded students

用法解析

well-rounded 在英语里的含义是 having a variety of experiences and abilities and a fully developed personality，well-rounded students 是指"全面发展的学生"，这种学生具备多种兴趣和技能。

实用语境

Why do you think it is beneficial for students to participate in extracurricular activities?

为什么你认为参加课外活动对学生有益？

Engaging in extracurricular activities is highly beneficial as it helps to develop *well-rounded students*. These activities provide opportunities for students to explore and discover their interests and passions outside of the academic realm. By participating in sports, clubs, or artistic endeavors, they can develop new skills, cultivate their talents, and uncover hidden strengths.

参与课外活动是非常有益的，因为它有助于培养全面发展的学生（well-rounded students）。这些活动为学生提供了在学术领域之外探索和发现自己的兴趣和爱好的机会。通过参加体育、俱乐部或艺术活动，他们可以发展新的技能，培养自己的才能，并发掘自身的优势。

08 spend quality time with

quality time 是一个固定词组，意思相当于 time spent giving your full attention to somebody, especially to your children after work，即"（用于全心照顾某人的）宝贵时光，优质时间"。spend quality time with somebody 是家庭教育话题中的万能表达，常见的搭配为：... spend quality time with his/her children。

用法解析

What do you think is the most important thing parents can do for their children?
你认为父母能为孩子做的最重要的事情是什么？

实用语境

I think it's important for parents to *spend quality time with* their children. By doing so, parents can connect with their children on a deeper level, understand their needs, and provide necessary guidance and support. Spending quality time with children also creates a sense of belonging within the family unit, which contributes to a child's overall well-being.

我认为父母与孩子共度美好时光（spend quality time with）是很重要的。通过这样做，父母可以和孩子建立深层次的连接，了解他们的需求，并提供必要的指导和支持。与孩子共度美好时光还能在家庭中创造一种归属感，这有助于提高孩子的整体幸福感。

09 be free from distractions

用法解析

be free from something 的意思是"摆脱了某事物，不包含某事物"，比如 free from pollution（远离污染），free from artificial colours and flavourings（不含人工色素和人工调味料）。短语 be free from distractions 的意思是"摆脱干扰"，在讨论学习环境时经常用到该表达。

实用语境

What do you think are the characteristics of a good learning environment?
你认为一个良好的学习环境都有哪些特征?

A good learning environment should be conducive to learning. It should be comfortable, well-lit, and *free from distractions*. It should also be equipped with the necessary resources, such as books, computers, and other learning materials.

一个良好的学习环境应该有利于学习。它应该是舒适的，光线充足的，并且不受干扰（free from distractions）。它还应该配备必要的资源，如书籍、电脑和其他学习材料。

10 learn at your own pace

do something at your own pace 的意思是"以适合自己的节奏做某事", learn at your own pace 即"按自己的节奏学习"。在讨论在线教育以及自学的好处时经常会用上这一短语。

What do you think are the benefits of online learning?
你认为在线学习有哪些好处?

I think the main benefit of online learning is that it's more flexible than traditional classroom learning, because it allows students to *learn at their own pace* and from anywhere in the world, as long as there is an internet connection. Online learning is also more affordable than traditional classroom learning, as it does away with many additional expenses such as transportation costs and course materials.

我认为在线学习的主要好处是,它比传统的课堂学习更灵活,因为它允许学生按照自己的节奏学习(learn at their own pace)。学生可以在全球任何地方学习,只要有网络连接。在线学习也比传统课堂学习更实惠,因为它省去了许多额外的费用,如交通费用和课程材料费用。

11 age-appropriate

用法解析

age-appropriate 是一个地道的口语表达，它的意思是"与年龄相符的"，比如 age-appropriate toys，它的意思相当于 toys that are appropriate to the age of the children。其他常见搭配还有 age-appropriate books/movies/outfits，在涉及儿童相关话题时可以用上它。

实用语境

Do you think parents should control what their children watch on TV?
你认为父母应该控制孩子观看的电视内容吗?

Yes, I strongly believe that parental guidance is essential when it comes to children's TV viewing habits. Parents should not only monitor the amount of time their children spend in front of the TV but also ensure that the programs they watch are *age-appropriate* and educational. They should also encourage their children to engage in other activities such as reading, playing outdoors, and interacting with peers.

是的，我坚信在孩子的电视观看习惯方面，家长的指导至关重要。家长不仅要留意孩子在电视机前的时间，还要确保他们观看的节目适合他们的年龄（age-appropriate）并具有教育意义。他们还应鼓励孩子参与其他活动，如阅读、户外活动和与同伴交流。

12 positive reinforcement

positive reinforcement 的意思是"正向激励",这是指给予某人表扬或奖励后,他们会继续表现得很好。与之相关的说法则是 negative reinforcement(负向激励),这是指给予某人惩罚或批评后,他们就会改正以免再次受到惩罚。这两个说法在教育方式相关话题中经常出现。

用法解析

What do you think is the most effective way to motivate students to study?
你认为激励学生学习最有效的方法是什么?

实用语境

Well, I believe that *positive reinforcement* is a powerful tool for motivating students. Instead of punishing students for not doing well, teachers should praise and reward students when they make progress or do a good job.

我认为正向激励（positive reinforcement）是激励学生的有力工具。教师不应该因为学生做得不好而惩罚他们，而应该在学生取得进步或做得好的时候表扬和奖励他们。

13 distract somebody from their studies

用法解析

distract somebody from something 的意思是"使某人在某事上分心"，比如：You're distracting me from my work. 你使我不能专心工作。distract somebody from their studies 即"使某人在学习上分心"，短语的被动形式为 Somebody is distracted from their studies。

实用语境

Do you think that schools should provide extracurricular activities for students?
你认为学校应该为学生提供课外活动吗？

Yes, I think schools should provide students with extracurricular activities like sports and music. These activities can help students develop their interests and skills outside of the classroom. However, schools should be careful not to provide too many activities that could *distract students from their studies*.

是的，我认为学校应该为学生提供体育和音乐等课外活动。这些活动可以帮助学生在课堂之外发展他们的兴趣和技能。然而，学校应注意不要提供太多的活动，以免分散学生在学习上的注意力（distract students from their studies）。

14 rote memorization

rote memorization 即我们常说的"死记硬背"，它也可以说成 rote learning，比如：the rote learning of facts 对事实的死记硬背。该短语对应的动词形式是 learn something by rote，比如：Children still learn their times tables by rote. 孩子们仍然靠死记硬背来学习乘法表。

用法解析

How do you think the education system has evolved over the years?
你认为这些年来教育系统发生了哪些变化?

实用语境

Well, the education system has certainly undergone significant changes. In the past, it was more traditional, with a focus on *rote memorization* and less practical learning. Nowadays, it's become more student-centered, encouraging critical thinking and problem-solving skills.

教育系统确实发生了重大变化。过去的教育比较传统，注重死记硬背（rote memorization），实践性学习较少。如今，它变得更加以学生为中心，鼓励批判性思维和解决问题的能力。

15 delve deep into a field of somebody's interest

用法解析

delve 的意思是"探索,探寻",比如:This biography delves deep into the artist's private life. 该传记深入探讨了这名艺术家的私生活。短语 delve deep into a field of somebody's interest 的意思是"深入探索某人感兴趣的领域"。

实用语境

Can you share your views on the importance of higher education?

你能谈谈你对高等教育重要性的看法吗?

Certainly. I believe that higher education is of paramount importance in today's world. It provides people with an opportunity to *delve deep into a field of their interest*, thereby gaining a comprehensive understanding of the subject matter. This not only equips them with specialized knowledge but also fosters the development of critical thinking and problem-solving skills.

当然可以。我认为高等教育在当今世界至关重要。它为人们提供了一个深入研究自己感兴趣领域(delve deep into a field of somebody's interest)的机会,从而获得对某一主题的全面理解。这不仅能让他们掌握专业知识,还能培养批判性思维和解决问题的能力。

16 instill good values in somebody

用法解析

instill something in somebody 的意思是"向某人灌输某事物（比如某种思想、行为方式或感受）"。短语 instill good values in somebody 即表示"向某人灌输优秀的品质"，这一表达在家庭教育和学校教育话题中经常出现。

实用语境

What role do you think parents play in a child's educational success?
你认为父母在孩子的教育成功中扮演什么角色？

Parents play a crucial role in a child's educational success. They are their child's first teachers and they *instill good values in their children*. Parents can support their child's education by showing an interest in their schoolwork, helping them with homework, and encouraging a love for learning. Moreover, parents can also influence their child's attitude towards education by setting a good example and demonstrating the value of knowledge and education.

父母对孩子的教育成功起着至关重要的作用。他们是孩子的第一任老师，向孩子灌输良好的价值观（instill good values in their children）。父母可以通过关心孩子的学业、帮助他们完成家庭作业以及鼓励他们热爱学习来支持孩子的教育。此外，父母还可以通过树立良好的榜样，展示知识和教育的价值，从而影响孩子对教育的态度。

17 set a positive example for somebody

用法解析 该短语的意思是"为某人树立一个正面的榜样"，常用于家庭教育话题中。该短语也可以说成 set a good example for somebody。

实用语境 How important is it for both parents to share the responsibility of raising a child?
父母双方共同承担抚养孩子的责任有多重要?

It's extremely important for both parents to share the responsibility of raising a child. Parenting is not just about providing for a child's physical needs but also about contributing to their emotional, social, and intellectual development. When both parents are involved, it not only lightens the load but also provides the child with different perspectives and role models. Moreover, shared parenting can foster equality within the home and *set a positive example for the child*.

父母双方共同承担养育子女的责任，这一点极其重要。养育孩子不仅仅是为了满足孩子的生理需求，也是为了促进孩子的情感、社交和智力发展。如果父母双方都参与其中，不仅能减轻孩子的负担，还能为孩子提供不同的视角和榜样。此外，共同养育还能促进家庭内部的平等，为孩子树立积极的榜样（set a positive example for somebody）。

18 culture shock

culture shock 的意思是"文化冲击"，它通常是指去异国或异地时产生的焦虑、孤独和困惑感，比如：Foreign students often experience culture shock when they first come to the U.S. 外国学生初到美国时往往会遭遇文化冲击。

 用法解析

Are there any potential drawbacks to studying abroad?
出国留学有什么潜在的缺点吗？

 实用语境

Yes, studying abroad does come with its own set of challenges. Firstly, students might face language barriers that can affect their academic performance and social interactions. They might also experience homesickness or *culture shock*, which can impact their mental health. Finally, studying abroad can be quite expensive. The cost of tuition, accommodation, and living expenses in a foreign country can be higher than in their home country.

是的，出国留学确实会带来一系列挑战。首先，学生可能会面临语言障碍，这会影响他们的学习成绩和社会交往。他们还可能会想家或受到文化冲击（culture shock），从而影响心理健康。最后，留学费用可能相当昂贵。国外的学费、住宿费和生活费都比国内的高。

19 something is tailored specifically to somebody

用法解析

该表达的意思是"某事物专门为某人定制"，比如目前一个教育趋势是强调"个性化学习"，该用法就可以用在相关表达中，比如：Classes/Teaching methods/Learning materials are tailored specifically to students. 课程／教学方法／学习资料是专门为学生们定制的。

实用语境

Why do some people prefer single-sex schools?
为什么有些人喜欢单性别学校？

There are several reasons why some people might prefer single-sex schools. One reason could be that they believe single-sex schools eliminate distractions and help students focus better on their studies. Some also argue that teaching methods in such schools can *be tailored specifically to* boys or girls, which can enhance learning.

有些人喜欢单性别学校，这背后有几个原因。其中一个原因可能是，他们认为单性别学校可以消除干扰，帮助学生更好地集中精力学习。有些人还认为，单性别学校可以根据男生或女生的具体情况制订教学方法（be tailored specifically to），从而提升学习效果。

20 be conducive to learning

be conducive to something 的意思是"有助于某事，有利于某事"，be conducive to learning 即表示"有利于学习"，该短语常见的搭配为：an atmosphere/environment that is conducive to learning（一个适合学习的氛围 / 环境）。

Do you think technology can replace teachers?
你认为技术可以取代教师吗?

While technology can supplement the role of teachers by providing a wealth of resources and interactive learning tools, I don't believe it can replace the human interaction and guidance that teachers provide. Teachers play a crucial role in motivating students, addressing their individual needs, and creating an environment that *is conducive to learning*.

虽然技术可以通过提供丰富的资源和互动学习工具来补充教师的作用，但我不认为技术可以取代教师所提供的人际互动和指导。教师在激励学生、满足学生的个性化需求以及创造有利于学习的环境方面（be conducive to learning）发挥着至关重要的作用。

21 something is a form of escapism

 用法解析

escapism 的意思是"逃避现实的消遣活动"，这样的活动包括阅读、看电影、度假等。比如我们可以说：For many people reading is a form of escapism. 对很多人来说，阅读是一种消遣放松的方式。注意 escapism 是不可数名词，前面不用加冠词。

 实用语境

Why do you think people enjoy reading?
你认为人们为什么喜欢阅读？

People enjoy reading for a multitude of reasons. For some, it's *a form of escapism*. A good book can transport you to different worlds and let you experience life through different perspectives. It's a great way to unwind after a long day. For others, reading is about learning and personal growth. It allows them to gain knowledge about various subjects, understand different cultures, and broaden their horizons.

人们喜欢阅读的原因多种多样。对有些人来说，这是一种逃避现实的消遣活动（a form of escapism）。一本好书可以把你带到不同的世界，让你从不同的角度体验生活。这是在漫长的一天之后放松身心的好方法。对其他人来说，读书是为了学习和个人成长。阅读让他们获得各种学科的知识，了解不同文化，开阔视野。

扫一扫，听录音

Part 6

工作话题

[01] hone somebody's skills
[02] recharge your batteries
[03] transferable skills
[04] spread yourself too thin
[05] upskill
[06] be available 24/7
[07] build up contacts
[08] excel at/in something
[09] something is aligned with somebody's interests
[10] have a diverse skill set
[11] grow personally and professionally
[12] be in high demand
[13] work around the clock
[14] build a close rapport with somebody
[15] enhance somebody's job prospects
[16] stand out in a competitive job market
[17] a glass ceiling
[18] a competitive edge
[19] stay relevant
[20] job hopping
[21] people skills
[22] professional etiquette
[23] create a good impression on somebody
[24] open doors to something
[25] juggle work and study
[26] wear many hats

01 hone somebody's skills

用法解析

hone somebody's skills 是一个在工作类话题中经常出现的说法，意思是"磨练某人的技能"，它可以代替常见说法 improve somebody's skills。

实用语境

Do you think it's important for people to continue learning after they finish school?

你认为人们在完成学业后继续学习重要吗？

Absolutely. I believe that lifelong learning is essential for personal growth and professional development. In today's fast-paced world, it's important to keep up with the latest trends and *hone your professional skills* to stay competitive in the job market.

当然重要。我认为终身学习对个人成长和职业发展至关重要。在当今这个快节奏的世界里，很重要的一点是要紧跟最新潮流，磨练专业技能（hone somebody's skills），以保持在就业市场上的竞争力。

02 recharge your batteries

recharge your batteries 是一个固定搭配，它的字面意思是"为电池充电"，引申为"休息（放松）以恢复精力"，注意 batteries 要用复数形式。

Do you think it's important to take time off work?
你认为从工作中抽时间休息重要吗？

Yes, I think it's important to take breaks during the day to *recharge your batteries*. If you work for too long without taking a break, you can become tired and less productive. Taking time off work can help you clear your mind and come back to your tasks with renewed energy and focus.

是的，我认为在一天中多休息是很重要的，这能够让你恢复精力（recharge your batteries）。如果你工作太久而不休息，你会变得很累，工作效率也会降低。花时间休息可以帮助你理清思路，这样继续工作时精力和注意力会更好。

03 | transferable skills

 用法解析

transferable skills 即人们常说的"可迁移性技能"，比如沟通技能、团队合作技能以及领导技能都属于可迁移技能。拥有这些技能的人在职场上会更受欢迎。

 实用语境

What skills do you think are most valuable in today's job market?
你认为哪些技能在当今的就业市场上最有价值？

I believe that *transferable skills* are highly valuable in the workplace today. These are skills that can be applied across different professions and industries, making individuals adaptable and versatile. Some examples of transferable skills include communication, problem-solving, teamwork, and leadership skills.

我认为可迁移性技能（transferable skills）在今天的职场是非常有价值的。这些技能可以应用于不同的专业和行业，使个人具有适应性且多才多艺。可迁移性技能包括沟通技能、问题解决技能、团队合作技能和领导技能。

04 spread yourself too thin

spread yourself too thin 是一个固定短语，意思是"同时做太多事情（以致没有足够时间或精力关注其中之一）"，在涉及工作效率的话题时可以用上该表达，比如：I realised I'd been spreading myself too thin so I resigned as secretary of the golf club. 我发觉我做的事情太多，因此辞去了高尔夫球俱乐部秘书一职。

用法解析

How can people prioritize their tasks when they are busy?
人们在忙碌时如何确定任务的轻重缓急？

实用语境

I think people should not *spread themselves too thin* by doing more than they can handle. To improve productivity, they can evaluate the urgency and importance of each task and finish the tasks based on their deadlines and significance. By doing this, they can focus on the most critical tasks and ensure they receive the necessary attention.

我认为人们不应该做超出自己能力范围的事情，这样会让自己应接不暇（spread themselves too thin）。为了提高工作效率，他们可以评估每项任务的紧迫性和重要性，并根据这些任务的最后期限和重要性来完成它们。通过这样做，他们可以专注于最关键的任务，确保这些任务得到必要的关注。

05 upskill

用法解析

upskill 的意思是"提升技能"，可以作及物动词也可作不及物动词使用。比如"我们正在提升这个团队的技能"，可以说：We are upskilling the team. 要表达"某人希望提升技能"，可以说 Somebody wants to upskill 或者 Somebody wishes to upskill，此时 upskill 是不及物动词。其名词形式是 upskilling。

实用语境

How do you think people can improve their job competitiveness?
你认为人们应该如何提升他们的职场竞争力？

I think continuous learning and *upskilling* can help people stay competitive in the job market. People should embrace a growth mindset and actively seek opportunities to expand their knowledge and acquire new skills. For example, they can attend workshops, seminars, or enroll in online courses to stay updated with the latest industry trends and technologies.

我认为不断学习和提高技能（upskilling）可以帮助人们在就业市场上保持竞争力。人们应该保持成长性心态，积极寻找机会去拓宽知识以及学习新技能。例如，他们可以参加工作坊、研讨会或在线课程，以跟上最新的行业趋势和技术。

06 be available 24/7

该短语里面的 24/7 即表示：24 hours a day, 7 days a week，引申为"全天候的"。比如：Having a kid is a 24/7 job. 照顾小孩是一个全天候工作。随着智能手机和即时通信软件的兴起，人们会发现即使下班时间也要处理工作，根本没有真正的休假。这种情况就可以说：People are expected to be available 24/7.

Do you think people are too busy these days?
你认为今天的人们过于忙碌吗？

Yes, I do. With the rise of social media and technology, people are expected to *be available 24/7*. This can make them feel overwhelmed, leading to burnout, anxiety, and other health problems.

是的，我是这么认为的。随着社交媒体和技术的兴起，人们被要求全天候工作（be available 24/7）。这可能会让他们感到不堪重负，从而导致倦怠、焦虑和其他健康问题。

07 | build up contacts

用法解析

contact 除了可以表示"接触，联系"之外，还可以表示"人脉，社会关系"。比如：He has a lot of good contacts in the music industry. 他在音乐界有很多人脉。build up contacts 即表示"建立人脉"。

实用语境

How do you think networking can contribute to career success?

你认为人际关系如何助力事业成功？

I believe that networking plays a crucial role in career success as it provides opportunities to connect with professionals in the industry, exchange knowledge, and *build up contacts*. By attending industry events, conferences, and seminars, people can establish valuable connections that can lead to new opportunities and career growth.

我认为人际关系在事业成功中发挥着至关重要的作用，因为它提供了与业内专业人士联系、交流知识和建立人脉（build up contacts）的机会。通过参加行业活动、行业会议和研讨会，人们可以建立有价值的联系，从而获得新的机遇和职业成长。

08 excel at/in something

excel 此处作为不及物动词使用，构成搭配 excel in/at something，意思是"擅长某事"。比如"擅长你的工作"，可以说：excel at your job。excel 也可以单独使用，比如：Academically he began to excel. 他开始在学术上出类拔萃。

用法解析

What qualities do you think are essential for achieving career success?
你认为哪些品质对于事业成功至关重要？

实用语境

I believe that determination and perseverance are crucial qualities for achieving career success. It's important to stay committed to one's goals, even in the face of challenges or setbacks. In fact, those who learn quickly and put in a lot of hard work are more likely to *excel at* their jobs.

我认为决心和毅力是事业成功的关键品质。即使面对挑战或挫折，也要坚持自己的目标。事实上，那些努力工作、快速学习的人更有可能在工作中取得优异成绩（excel at their jobs）。

09 something is aligned with somebody's interests

A is aligned with B 的意思是 "A 与 B 保持一致"，比如：This policy is closely aligned with the goals of the organization. 这一方针与该机构的目标非常一致。something is aligned with somebody's interests 即表示 "某事物与某人的兴趣爱好一致"，在讨论选择工作或者报考专业时我们都可以用上这一说法。

What is the most important thing to consider when choosing a career?
在选择职业时，最重要的考虑因素是什么？

I think it is important for people to choose a job that is *aligned with their interests* because it can help them feel more fulfilled and motivated in their work. For example, if someone is interested in art and they work in a creative field like graphic design or advertising, they may be more likely to enjoy their job and improve their job-related skills.

我认为选择一份与人们兴趣相符（aligned with their interests）的工作非常重要，因为这可以让他们在工作中感到更充实、更有动力。例如，如果某人对艺术感兴趣，并且能在平面设计或广告等创意领域工作，那么这个人可能会更享受自己的工作，并更有可能提升与工作相关的技能。

10 have a diverse skill set

a skill set 的意思相当于 a person's range of skills or abilities（个人技能表），have a diverse skill set 即表示"拥有多种技能组合"。在形容某人具有多种技能时，我们就可以说：Somebody has a diverse skill set.

用法解析

Do you think people should be encouraged to develop a wide range of skills?
你认为应该鼓励人们发展各种技能吗?

实用语境

Yes, I think it's important to *have a diverse skill set* because it can help you adjust to different situations and be more versatile in your career. For example, if you're a software engineer who are proficient in multiple programming languages, you can work on a wider range of projects and be more valuable to your employer.

是的，我认为拥有多样化的技能组合（have a diverse skill set）非常重要，因为这可以帮你适应不同的情况，并且在你的职业生涯中更加多面。举个例子，如果你是一名精通多种编程语言的软件工程师，你就可以参与更多类型的项目，变得更有价值。

11 grow personally and professionally

professional 除了可以表示"专业的，内行的"，还可以表示"职业的，工作的"，比如：professional contacts 意为"工作上的熟人"。短语 grow personally and professionally 即表示"在生活和工作上获得成长"。

How important do you think it is for individuals to continue learning throughout their careers?
你认为个人在职业生涯中不断学习有多重要?

I think lifelong learning is paramount for people's career advancement. In today's ever-evolving world, new technologies and knowledge emerge constantly. By continuously acquiring new skills and knowledge, people can stay updated, adapt to industry changes, and *grow personally and professionally*.

我认为终身学习对人们的职业发展至关重要。在当今不断发展的世界中，新技术和新知识层出不穷。通过不断学习新技能和新知识，人们可以保持与时俱进，适应行业变化，以及在生活和工作上获得成长（grow personally and professionally）。

12 be in high demand

Something is in high demand 的意思是"人们对某事物有很大的需求"。在职场话题中可以用来说明高素质人才或者某些工作技能处于供不应求的状态。同义表达还有 Something is highly sought after。

用法解析

What jobs do you think are popular in your country?
你认为哪些工作在你们国家比较流行?

实用语境

I think jobs in the technology sector are popular. For example, software developers and data analysts are highly sought after by tech firms. In addition, healthcare professionals such as doctors and nurses are also *in high demand* due to population ageing.

我认为技术领域的工作很受欢迎。例如,软件开发人员和数据分析师是科技公司的抢手人才。此外,由于人口老龄化,医生和护士等医疗保健专业人员的需求量也很大(in high demand)。

13 work around the clock

用法解析

around the clock 相当于 all day and all night（夜以继日），work around the clock 即"昼夜不停地工作"。同义表达还有 work non-stop 以及 work long hours。

实用语境

What kinds of jobs do you think are demanding?
你认为哪些工作比较耗费精力？

I think jobs in hotels, restaurants, and resorts are demanding because they often require employees to work long hours, especially during peak seasons or holidays. The staff needs to ensure that guests are taken good care of and their needs are met, which sometimes means they have to *work around the clock*.

我认为酒店、餐馆和景区的工作很耗费精力，因为它们经常需要员工长时间工作，尤其是在旺季或节假日期间。员工需要确保客人得到很好的照顾并且他们的需求得到满足，这有时意味着员工需要夜以继日地工作（work around the clock）。

14　build a close rapport with somebody

该短语的含义为"与某人建立融洽的关系"，在涉及人际关系话题时经常可以用上该表达。它可以用来代替常见说法 develop a close relationship with somebody。

用法解析

What are some of the most important qualities that you think a good manager should have?
你认为优秀的管理者应具备哪些最重要的素质？

实用语境

I think that a good manager should be able to *build a close rapport with* their team members. This means that they should be able to communicate effectively and be approachable. They should also be able to provide constructive feedback and support their team members in achieving their goals.

我认为一名优秀的经理应该能够与团队成员建立密切的关系（build a close rapport with somebody）。这意味着他们要能够有效沟通且平易近人。他们还应该能够提供建设性的反馈意见，并支持团队成员实现他们的目标。

15 enhance somebody's job prospects

prospects 的意思是"前景，前途"，比如：I had no job, no education, and no prospects. 我没有工作，没受过什么教育，前途渺茫。短语 enhance somebody's job prospects 即"提升某人的工作前景"，注意 prospects 必须用复数形式。

Do you think it's important for people to have a clear career path?
你认为清晰的职业道路对人们来说重要吗？

Yes, I do. Having a clear career path can help people focus on what they want to achieve and make better decisions about their education and training. It can also help them identify opportunities that will *enhance their job prospects.*

是的，我是这样认为的。拥有清晰的职业发展道路可以帮助人们专注于自己想要实现的目标，并帮助人们在教育和培训方面做出更好的决定。它还可以帮助他们发现能够改善其工作前景（enhance their job prospects）的机会。

16 stand out in a competitive job market

stand out的字面意思是"站起来",引申为"脱颖而出", 例句: That day still stands out as the greatest day in my life. 那天仍是我一生中最美好的日子。本例短语 的含义为"在竞争激烈的职场中脱颖而出"。

How can job seekers make themselves more attractive to potential employers?
求职者如何让自己对潜在雇主更具吸引力?

I think one way job seekers can improve their employability is to take courses that help them develop new skills. This shows that they are dedicated to learning and growing as a professional. It's also important to tailor their resume and cover letter to each job they apply for. This highlights their relevant experience and skills and helps them *stand out in a competitive job market.*

我认为求职者提高就业能力的一个方法就是参加 有助于他们发展新技能的课程。这表明他们致力 于学习成长为一名专业人士。同样重要的是,求 职者应根据自己申请的每份工作量身定制简历和 求职信。这可以突出他们的相关经验和技能,帮 助他们在竞争激烈的就业市场中脱颖而出(stand out in a competitive job market)。

17 a glass ceiling

用法解析

a glass ceiling 即我们常说的"玻璃天花板"，它通常指女性或某一群体的人在职务晋升上遇到的无形障碍。常见的搭配为 hit/break/shatter the glass ceiling（打破玻璃天花板）。

实用语境

What do you think are some of the disadvantages of working in a large company?
你认为在大公司工作有哪些缺点？

I think one of the drawbacks of working in a large company is that you have to spend a lot of time dealing with office politics. In large companies, there is also *a glass ceiling* for people who are from disadvantaged backgrounds. They may not have access to the same resources or connections as people who come from more privileged backgrounds.

我认为在大公司工作的一个缺点是你必须花费大量时间处理办公室政治。在大公司，出身不利的人也会面临"玻璃天花板"（a glass ceiling）。他们可能无法获得与出身优越者相同的资源或关系。

18 a competitive edge

单词 edge 可以表示"优势"，比如：Companies are employing more research teams to get an edge. 公司在雇用更多的研究小组以占据优势。a competitive edge 意思即"竞争优势"，该短语的常见搭配为 have/gain a competitive edge over somebody（与某人相比具有竞争优势）。

用法解析

What kind of jobs do you think will be popular in the future?
你认为哪种工作在未来会受欢迎？

实用语境

I think tech jobs will be popular in the future because we are now entering a digital age. Jobs like software development and data analysis are highly sought after by employers. By acquiring knowledge and skills related to the tech industry, people can gain *a competitive edge* in the job market.

我认为技术工作在未来会很受欢迎，因为我们正在进入一个数字时代。软件开发和数据分析等工作备受雇主青睐。通过积累与科技行业相关的知识和技能，人们可以在就业市场上获得竞争优势（a competitive edge）。

19 stay relevant

用法解析

relevant 除了表示"相关的，有关的"，还可以表示"重要的，有价值的"，比如：Her novel is still relevant today. 她的小说至今仍很有价值。stay relevant 也是职场话题中经常出现的一个表达，它相当于"与时俱进，保持自己的价值"。relevant 的名词形式 relevance 也具有"重要性，价值"含义。

实用语境

What can people do to increase their competitiveness in today's job market?

人们应该怎样做才能提高自己在当今就业市场上的竞争力？

I think it's important for people to keep up with the latest trends and technologies in their field. This will help them *stay relevant* in today's job market. For example, if you're in the tech industry, you should be familiar with programming languages and software development tools that are currently in demand. Additionally, soft skills such as communication and teamwork skills are also important for success in any job.

我认为人们必须跟上其所在领域的最新趋势和技术。这将有助于他们在当今的就业市场中保持竞争力（stay relevant）。例如，如果你从事的是技术行业，那么你就应该熟悉目前最热门的编程语言和软件开发工具。此外，沟通和团队合作等软技能对于取得职场成功也很重要。

20 job hopping

job hopping 的意思是"跳槽"，这是一个名词，如果是动词表达则可以说 somebody job-hops，比如：Young people are more likely to job-hop than their older counterparts. 年轻人比起上一代人更容易跳槽。要描述"一个经常跳槽的人"，则可以说 a job-hopper。

用法解析

Do you think people today change jobs more often than in the past?
你认为现在的人比过去更频繁地更换工作吗？

实用语境

Yes, in previous generations, it was common for individuals to stay with one company for their entire working life. However, with the rapid pace of technological advancement, employees now have more options and opportunities available to them. This has led to an increase in *job hopping* as employees seek out these new opportunities.

是的，在上一代人中，整个职业生涯都在一家公司是很常见的。然而，随着技术的飞速发展，员工现在有了更多的选择和机会。这导致跳槽现象（job hopping）增多，因为员工要寻找这些新机会。

21 people skills

用法解析

people skills 的意思是"人际交往技巧",比如: Good people skills are important in customer service. 良好的人际交往技巧对客户服务非常重要。people skills 可以替换常见说法 interpersonal skills。要形容一个善于交际的人,还可以说 a people person。

实用语境

In your opinion, what qualities do employers generally seek in a job candidate?
在你看来,雇主一般看重求职者身上哪些素质?

Employers typically look for a blend of hard and soft skills in a candidate. Hard skills are job-specific abilities or knowledge acquired through education, training, or experience. These could include proficiency in a foreign language, computer programming skills, or expertise in project management. On the other hand, soft skills are more general and can be applied to any job. These include *people skills*, teamwork skills, adaptability, and so on.

雇主通常希望求职者具备软硬两种技能。硬技能是通过教育、培训或经验获得的与工作相关的能力或知识。这些技能包括熟练掌握一门外语、计算机编程技能或项目管理方面的专业知识。另一方面,软技能更具通用性,可适用于任何工作。这些技能包括人际交往技能(people skills)、团队合作技能、适应能力等。

22 professional etiquette

professional etiquette 是个固定短语，意思是"行业规范，行业规矩"，比如：The solicitor was accused of a breach of professional etiquette. 该律师被指控违反了行业规矩。

Are internships important for students?
实习对学生来说重要吗？

Internships are crucial for students as they provide practical experience in a professional environment. They offer students an opportunity to apply the theoretical knowledge they have gained in their academic studies. Internships also help students understand the dynamics of the workplace, learn *professional etiquette*, and develop networking skills.

实习对于学生来说至关重要，因为实习可以提供在专业环境中的实践经验。实习为学生提供了应用所学理论知识的机会。实习还能帮助学生了解工作场所的情况，学习行业规范（professional etiquette），发展人际交往技能。

23 create a good impression on somebody

用法解析

该短语意为"给某人创造良好的印象"，比如：As a serious candidate, you want to create a good impression on everyone you meet. 作为一名认真的候选人，你希望给遇到的每个人都留下好印象。本例短语也可以说成 make a good impression on somebody。

实用语境

How important do you think it is to have a good CV when applying for jobs?
你认为求职时拥有一份好的简历有多重要？

I believe having a well-crafted CV is absolutely crucial when applying for jobs, because it will help you *create a good impression on* employers. It also provides a snapshot of your skills, experiences, and achievements. A good CV should be clear, concise, and tailored to the specific role one is applying for. It should highlight relevant skills and experiences that align with the job requirements.

我认为拥有一份精心制作的简历在求职时绝对是至关重要的，因为它能帮助你给雇主留下良好的印象（create a good impression on）。同时，简历也是你的技能、经验和成就的缩影。一份好的简历应该清晰、简洁，并针对所申请的具体职位量身定制。简历应突出与职位要求相符的相关技能和经验。

24 open doors to something

该短语的意思相当于 make something possible，即"为某事创造机会"，比如要表达"社交活动能创造更多的职业机会"，可以说：Networking can open doors to more professional opportunities. 人际交往可以打开通往更多职业机会的大门。

用法解析

How can internships influence a student's career choices?
实习如何影响学生的职业选择?

实用语境

Internships can greatly influence a student's career choices. They provide a glimpse into a particular industry or job role, helping students understand what it entails. This experience can either reinforce their interest in their chosen field or prompt them to explore other options. Furthermore, internships can *open doors to* future job opportunities in the same organization or industry.

实习可以极大地影响学生的职业选择。实习可以让学生了解特定行业或工作角色，帮助他们理解其要求。这种经历可以增强他们对所选领域的兴趣，也可以促使他们探索其他选择。此外，实习还能为今后在同一组织或行业工作创造机会（open doors to）。

25 | juggle work and study

用法解析

juggle A and B 表示"同时应对A和B两项活动",比如:
Many parents find it hard to juggle children and a career. 许多父母发现很难一边照顾孩子一边忙事业。
juggle work and study 即为"同时应对工作和学习"。

实用语境

How do you think part-time work can affect a student's studies?
你认为兼职工作会对学生的学习产生什么影响?

Part-time work can have both positive and negative impacts on a student's studies. On the positive side, it can enhance their time management and multitasking skills as they learn to *juggle work and study*. It also provides practical experiences that can complement their academic learning. On the flip side, if a student works too many hours, it could lead to fatigue and stress. This could interfere with their study time and potentially affect their academic performance. Therefore, it's crucial for students to strike a balance between their work and study.

兼职工作对学生的学习既有积极影响,也有消极影响。从积极的方面来说,兼职可以提高学生的时间管理能力和多任务处理能力,让他们学会如何同时应对工作和学习(juggle work and study)。它还能提供实践经验,对他们的学习起到补充作用。反之,如果学生工作时间过长,可能会导致疲劳和压力。这可能会影响他们的学习时间,并有可能影响他们的学习成绩。因此,学生必须在工作和学习之间取得平衡。

26 wear many hats

wear many hats 是一个短语，意思是"身兼多职"（to have many jobs or roles），比如：She wears many hats: she's a doctor, a musician, and a writer. 她身兼数职：医生、音乐家和作家。该短语也可以写成 wear multiple/several hats。

用法解析

Can you tell me about the advantages of working for a small company?
你能谈谈在小公司工作的优势吗？

实用语境

Certainly. One of the main advantages of working for a small company is that employees often have the opportunity to *wear many hats* and gain experience in different areas. This can lead to a more diverse skill set and potentially more opportunities for advancement. Additionally, in a small company, there's often a closer relationship between employees and management, which can lead to a more personal and supportive work environment.

当然可以。在小公司工作的一个主要优势是员工往往有机会在不同领域身兼数职（wear many hats），积累经验。这可以让员工掌握更多样化的技能，并有可能获得更多的晋升机会。此外，在小公司里，员工和管理层之间的关系往往更加密切，这可以营造一个更加人性化和相互支持的工作环境。

Part 7

環保話題

扫一扫,听录音

01 food miles
02 reduce somebody's carbon footprint
03 adopt sustainable practices in your daily life
04 eco-conscious
05 a throwaway society
06 make ... more accessible and affordable for everyone
07 plastic packaging
08 something ends up in landfills
09 something contributes to global warming
10 redress the ecological balance
11 do something at the expense of the environment
12 dispose of something
13 exhaust fumes
14 something leads to habitat loss for many species
15 something is a sustainable source of power
16 discharge untreated waste into rivers and oceans
17 coastal erosion
18 energy-efficient appliances
19 extreme weather events

01 food miles

用法解析

food miles 的意思是"食物里程"，这是指消费者与食物原产地之间的距离。食物里程远则意味着食物从产地运输到消费者手上需要导致更多的碳排放。如果购买本地产品，就可以减少食物里程。要表达"本地生产的农产品"，可以说 locally sourced produce。

实用语境

Do you think people should be more aware of where their food comes from?
你认为人们应该更加了解食物的来源吗？

Yes, I think so. People should try to lessen the environmental impact of food transportation by *reducing their food miles*. This can be done by buying locally sourced produce. People can also try growing their own vegetables at home, which will not only reduce food miles but also give them fresh produce right at their doorstep.

是的，我是这样认为的。人们应该通过减少他们的食物里程（reduce their food miles）来尽量降低食物运输对环境的影响。这可以通过购买本地农产品来实现。人们还可以尝试在家里自己种菜，这样不仅可以减少食物里程，还可以让他们在家门口就能获得新鲜的农产品。

02 reduce somebody's carbon footprint

carbon footprint 的意思是"碳足迹"，是指企业或个人通过交通运输、食品生产和消费以及各类生产过程引起的温室气体排放总量。reduce somebody's carbon footprint 也是环保话题中的万能表达，像植树、乘坐公共交通以及减少能源浪费等措施都能减少碳足迹。

用法解析

What do you think individuals can do to help protect the environment?
个人可以通过做什么来保护环境?

实用语境

There are many things individuals can do to help the environment. For example, they can use public transport instead of driving their own cars, and reduce their energy consumption by turning off lights and appliances when they're not in use. They can also support companies that are making an effort to *reduce their carbon footprint* by using renewable energy sources.

个人可以做很多事情来保护环境。例如，他们可以使用公共交通工具而不是自己开车，以及关掉不用的电灯和电器以减少能源消耗。他们还可以支持那些通过使用可再生能源来减少碳足迹的企业（reduce their carbon footprint）。

03 adopt sustainable practices in your daily life

用法解析

sustainable 的意思是"可持续的，不破坏环境的"，比如 Cycling is a totally sustainable form of transport. 骑自行车是一种很环保的交通方式。practice 此处表示"惯常做法"。短语 adopt sustainable practices in your daily life 意思是"在日常生活中实践环保的生活习惯"。

实用语境

How can people make a positive impact on the planet?
人们如何才能对地球产生积极影响？

I think one way people can help the environment is by conserving energy through using energy-efficient appliances. Additionally, they can reduce water waste and embrace renewable energy sources such as solar power and wind energy. Moreover, people can *adopt sustainable practices in their daily lives*, like composting organic waste and supporting eco-friendly businesses.

我认为，人们保护环境的一种方式是通过使用节能电器来节约能源。此外，人们还可以减少水资源浪费，使用太阳能和风能等可再生能源。此外，人们还可以在日常生活中实践环保的生活习惯（adopt sustainable practices in their daily lives），比如制作有机堆肥和支持环保型企业。

04 eco-conscious

XX-conscious 的意思是"有……意识的，对……敏感的"，比如 fashion-conscious（对时尚敏感的），health-conscious（有健康意识的）。eco-conscious 的意思是"有环保意识的"，同义表达还有 environmentally conscious，比如：eco-conscious consumers 有环保意识的消费者。

Do you think people should be more aware of environmental issues?
你认为人们应该更加关注环境问题吗?

Yes, I think people should be more *eco-conscious* because we depend on nature for our survival and well-being, and the destruction of nature can have a huge impact on our lives. For example, the loss of biodiversity is a serious issue that affects not only animals and plants but also humans. Therefore, it's important that we take care of the environment and preserve it for future generations.

是的,我认为人们应该更具生态意识(eco-conscious),因为我们的生存和福祉依赖于自然，而自然的破坏会对我们的生活产生巨大影响。例如，生物多样性的丧失是一个严重的问题，它不仅影响动植物，而且影响人类。因此，我们必须保护环境并为子孙后代保留一个好的环境。

05 a throwaway society

用法解析

throwaway 的意思是"用完丢弃的，一次性使用的"，
a throwaway society 即"充斥着一次性物品的社会"。
在涉及资源浪费以及回收等话题中可以用上该表达。

实用语境

Do you think people should be encouraged to
recycle more?
你认为应该鼓励人们更多地回收利用物品吗？

Absolutely. We live in *a throwaway society* where
people are too quick to throw things away instead of
finding ways to reuse them. For example, a lot of people
today prefer to replace faulty household appliances
than to repair them. By recycling more, we can help to
reduce waste and protect the environment.

当然。我们生活在一个用完即弃的社会（a
throwaway society）。人们很快就扔掉东西，而不
是尝试去重新利用它们。例如，今天很多人更喜
欢更换有故障的家用电器而不是修理它们。通过
更多地回收利用，我们可以帮助减少浪费并保护
环境。

06 make ... more accessible and affordable for everyone

该短语的意思是"让每个人能够更加方便和实惠地获得……"，在环保政策相关的话题中可以用上该短语。比如 make public transport more accessible and affordable for everyone, make renewable energy sources more accessible and affordable for everyone。

What can governments do to help the environment?
政府能做些什么来保护环境？

I think governments can introduce policies that encourage people and businesses to be more environmentally friendly. For example, they can offer tax incentives for companies that use renewable energy or reduce their carbon footprint. They can also invest in public transport and *make it more accessible and affordable for everyone*.

我认为政府可以出台政策，鼓励人们和企业变得更加环保。例如，他们可以为使用可再生能源或减少碳足迹的公司提供税收优惠。他们还可以投资公共交通，让每个人能够更加方便和实惠地获得它（make it more accessible and affordable for everyone）。

07 plastic packaging

 用法解析

plastic packaging 即"塑料包装",这是环保话题中的高频表达。塑料包装难以降解(decompose),会长期在环境中存在。目前塑料污染(plastic pollution)也是一个很严重的环境问题,而解决这一问题就要减少使用塑料包装,并鼓励人们使用可降解的材料(biodegradable materials)。

 实用语境

Do you think people are doing enough to protect the environment?
你认为人们在保护环境方面做得足够了吗?

No, I don't think so. There is still a lot more that can be done. For example, we should reduce our use of *plastic packaging*, which is a major contributor to environmental pollution. We can use reusable bags instead of plastic bags when we go shopping. We can also buy products that are packaged in biodegradable materials.

不,我不这么认为。人们还有很多事情可以做。例如,我们应该减少塑料包装(plastic packaging)的使用,它是环境污染的主要来源。购物时,我们可以使用可重复使用的袋子来代替塑料袋。我们还可以购买用可生物降解材料包装的产品。

08 something ends up in landfills

landfill 是指"垃圾填埋场"，something ends up in landfills 的意思是"某事物最终进入垃圾填埋场"。像电器和电池等有害垃圾如果不经处理直接就进入垃圾填埋场，会造成土壤以及水资源污染。

What can people do to reduce waste?
人们可以通过做些什么来减少浪费？

I think one effective approach is to practice recycling. By separating recyclable materials such as paper, plastic, and glass, we can ensure that they are processed and reused instead of being discarded and *ending up in landfills*.

我认为一种有效的方法是回收利用。通过对纸张、塑料和玻璃等可回收材料进行分类，我们可以确保它们得到处理和再利用，而不是被丢弃并最终进入垃圾填埋场（end up in landfills）。

09 something contributes to global warming

 用法解析

该短语的意思是"某事物导致了全球变暖",这是环保话题中的高频短语。导致全球变暖的原因通常是化石燃料的燃烧(the burning of fossil fuels)以及森林砍伐(deforestation)等。

 实用语境

Do you think humans have caused great damage to the environment?

你认为人类对环境造成了巨大破坏吗?

Yes, I do think so. Humans have caused serious damage to the planet. We have been cutting down trees and destroying wildlife habitats for decades. This has led to many species going extinct. We have also produced too many greenhouse gases, which *contribute to global warming*. All of this shows that we have greatly upset the ecosystem.

是的,我是这么认为的。人类对地球造成了严重破坏。数十年来,我们一直在砍伐树木,破坏野生动物的栖息地。这导致许多物种灭绝。我们还制造了太多温室气体,导致全球变暖(contribute to global warming)。所有这些都表明,我们极大地破坏了生态系统。

10 redress the ecological balance

redress the balance 的意思是"恢复平衡，恢复公平合理的情况"，redress the ecological balance 即"恢复生态系统平衡"。

What can governments do to promote environmental sustainability?
政府如何促进环境的可持续发展？

I think governments play a crucial role in promoting environmental sustainability. They can implement policies that encourage the use of renewable energy sources, invest in public transportation infrastructure to reduce reliance on private vehicles, and enforce stricter regulations on industrial emissions. By doing so, they can help *redress the ecological balance* and mitigate the harmful effects of human activities on the environment.

我认为政府在促进环境可持续性方面发挥着至关重要的作用。他们可以实施鼓励使用可再生能源的政策、投资公共交通基础设施以减少对私家车的依赖，并对工业排放实施更严格的法规。通过这样做，它们可以帮助恢复生态平衡（redress the ecological balance）并减轻人类活动对环境的有害影响。

11 do something at the expense of the environment

用法解析

at the expense of something 的意思是"以某事物为代价"，本例短语的意思即"以牺牲环境为代价做某事"，比如 develop the economy at the expense of the environment（以牺牲环境为代价发展经济）。该短语也可以说成 do something at the cost of the environment。

实用语境

How can businesses contribute to the environment?
企业如何为环境做出贡献？

I think businesses should be more mindful of their impact on the environment and take steps to reduce their carbon footprint. For example, they should reduce the use of plastic packaging because it can cause harm to wildlife and ecosystems. They can use naturally biodegradable materials as alternatives. It is important that businesses not focus on profits *at the expense of the environment*.

我认为，企业应该更加关注其对环境的影响，并采取措施减少碳足迹。例如，企业应减少塑料包装的使用，因为塑料包装会对野生动物和生态系统造成危害。他们可以使用可自然生物降解的材料作为替代品。重要的是，企业不能以牺牲环境为代价（at the expense of the environment）来获取利润。

12 | dispose of something

该短语的意思是"处理某事物"，比如"处理工业废品"可以说 dispose of industrial waste，注意 dispose 后面的介词 of 不能去掉。该短语的被动形式为 Something is disposed of，比如：The waste was not properly disposed of. 这些废品没有被妥善处理。

What are some of the major causes of pollution in urban areas?
造成城市地区污染的主要原因有哪些？

I think one of the main causes of pollution in urban areas is vehicle emissions. Cars and buses produce harmful gases such as carbon monoxide and nitrogen oxide, which contribute to air pollution. Another significant source is industrial waste. Many factories release pollutants into the air and the river without properly *disposing of* them, causing environmental contamination.

我认为城市污染的主要原因之一是汽车尾气排放。汽车和公共汽车会产生一氧化碳和氮氧化物等有害气体，导致空气污染。另一个重要污染源是工业废物。许多工厂将污染物排放到空气和河流中，而没有妥善处理（dispose of）它们，这造成了环境污染。

13 exhaust fumes

用法解析

exhaust fumes 的意思是"汽车尾气"，该短语也可以说成 exhaust gases，比如：The city's streets are filthy and choked with exhaust fumes/gases. 那座城市的街道肮脏不堪，弥漫着令人窒息的废气。

实用语境

What do you think are the main causes of air pollution?
你认为导致空气污染的主要因素都有哪些?

I think the main causes of air pollution are industrialization and urbanization. Factories emit harmful gases and vehicles *release exhaust fumes*, both of which contribute significantly to air pollution. Deforestation is another cause as trees absorb carbon dioxide and other pollutants.

我认为造成空气污染的主要原因是工业化和城市化。工厂排放有害气体，汽车排放尾气（release exhaust fumes），这些都是造成空气污染的重要原因。森林砍伐是另一个原因，因为树木会吸收二氧化碳和其他污染物。

14 something leads to habitat loss for many species

habitat 指的是"（动植物的）栖息地"，something leads to habitat loss for many species 即"某事物导致很多物种失去了栖息地"。造成栖息地减少的因素包括城市化、砍伐森林（deforestation）以及采矿（mining）等。

How does deforestation affect our environment and biodiversity?
砍伐森林如何影响我们的环境和生物多样性？

Deforestation has a profound impact on our environment and biodiversity. It *leads to habitat loss for many species*, which can result in their extinction. Moreover, trees absorb carbon dioxide, so their removal increases the amount of greenhouse gases in the atmosphere, contributing to climate change.

砍伐森林对我们的环境和生物多样性有着深远的影响。它导致许多物种失去栖息地（lead to habitat loss for many species），这可能导致这些物种灭绝。此外，树木会吸收二氧化碳，因此砍伐树木会增加大气中的温室气体含量，导致气候变化。

15 something is a sustainable source of power

 用法解析

该短语的意思是"某事物是一种可持续性能源"，我们可以用它来描述各种清洁能源，比如风能、太阳能和水电（hydroelectric power）都属于这种能源形式。

 实用语境

Do you think renewable energy is important?
你认为可再生能源重要吗？

Absolutely. Renewable energy is crucial because it's *a sustainable source of power* that doesn't deplete our planet's natural resources. Unlike fossil fuels, renewable energy sources like solar, wind, and hydroelectric power are virtually inexhaustible. Moreover, they emit significantly fewer greenhouse gases, which is beneficial for mitigating climate change.

当然重要。可再生能源之所以重要，是因为它是一种可持续能源（a sustainable source of power），它不会耗尽地球自然资源。与化石燃料不同，太阳能、风能和水电等可再生能源几乎取之不尽用之不竭。此外，它们排放的温室气体也少得多，有利于减缓气候变化。

16 discharge untreated waste into rivers and oceans

discharge something into ... 的意思是"将某事物排放到……"，比如：Sewage is discharged directly into the sea. 污水被直接排放到海里。discharge untreated waste into rivers and oceans 的含义是"将未处理的废物排放到河流和海洋中"，在描述工厂造成的污染时可以用上该表达。

用法解析

What do you think are the main causes of water pollution?
你认为导致水污染的主要原因是什么？

实用语境

There are several causes of water pollution. Industrial waste is a major contributor, as factories often *discharge untreated waste into rivers and oceans*. Agricultural runoff, which includes pesticides and fertilizers, also pollutes water bodies. Additionally, improper disposal of household waste and sewage can lead to water contamination.

水污染是由多种原因导致的。工业废料是主要原因之一，因为工厂经常向河流和海洋排放未经处理的废物（discharge untreated waste）。包含杀虫剂和化肥在内的农业径流也会污染水体。此外，生活垃圾和污水的不当处理也会导致水污染。

17 | coastal erosion

 用法解析

该短语的含义是"海岸侵蚀"，它也可以说成 marine erosion。海岸侵蚀是指海边的石头和土壤遭到海水侵蚀，造成海岸侵蚀的原因通常是海平面上升（rising sea levels）。

 实用语境

Can you discuss some of the potential impacts of rising sea levels?

你能谈谈海平面上升的一些潜在影响吗?

Certainly. Rising sea levels pose a significant threat to coastal communities around the world. They can lead to increased *coastal erosion*, more frequent and severe flooding, and loss of habitat for plants, fish, and birds. In some low-lying areas and small island nations, entire communities could be displaced.

当然可以。海平面上升对世界各地的沿海社区构成重大威胁。海平面上升会导致海岸侵蚀（coastal erosion）加剧，它还会导致更加频繁和严重的洪水，同时植物、鱼类和鸟类会失去栖息地。在一些低洼地区和小岛屿国家，整个社区都可能流离失所。

18 energy-efficient appliances

appliances 的意思是"家用电器",比如冰箱（refrigerator）、洗碗机（dishwasher）、微波炉（microwave oven）等。energy-efficient appliances 即"节能家电"。

用法解析

What steps can individuals take to promote the use of renewable energy?
个人可以采取哪些措施来推广可再生能源的使用？

实用语境

Individuals can play a significant role in promoting renewable energy. They can install solar panels on their homes or opt for green energy plans from their utility providers. They can also advocate for policies that support renewable energy development and use *energy-efficient appliances* to reduce their overall energy consumption.

个人可以在推广可再生能源方面发挥重要作用。他们可以在家中安装太阳能电池板，或选择公用事业供应商提供的绿色能源计划。他们还可以支持那些促进可再生能源发展的政策，并使用节能电器（energy-efficient appliances）来降低总体能耗。

19 extreme weather events

用法解析

该短语的意思是"极端天气事件",比如极端高温（record-breaking heat waves）、洪水以及长时间的干旱（droughts）。极端天气事件也是全球变暖的一个副作用。

实用语境

What are some impacts of melting ice caps on the environment?

冰盖融化对环境有哪些影响?

Melting ice caps can lead to a rise in sea levels, which can cause coastal flooding and loss of land. It also affects marine life as it changes the habitats of various species. Moreover, it can lead to more *extreme weather events* as it disrupts normal weather patterns.

冰盖融化会导致海平面上升,造成沿海洪水泛滥和土地流失。冰盖融化还会影响海洋生物,因为它会改变各种物种的栖息地。此外,冰盖融化还会扰乱正常的天气模式,导致更多极端天气事件（extreme weather events）的发生。

扫一扫，听录音

政府话题

Part 8

01 law-abiding citizens
02 act in the public interest
03 make the public aware of something
04 increase police presence
05 make amends for somebody's crimes
06 change somebody's ways
07 be high on the government's agenda
08 the public purse
09 improve social mobility
10 reintegrate into society
11 abuse somebody's power
12 provide financial incentives to something
13 provide a safety net for somebody
14 take care of the most vulnerable members of society
15 a level playing field
16 limit the marketing of junk food to children
17 drunk driving
18 foster a spirit of camaraderie and unity among nations

01 law-abiding citizens

用法解析

该短语的意思是"遵纪守法的公民"，由此衍生出一个说法是 abide by the law/rule，比如：You'll have to abide by the rules of the club. 你必须遵守俱乐部的规定。

实用语境

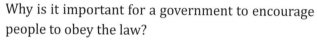

Why is it important for a government to encourage people to obey the law?
为什么政府必须鼓励人们遵守法律？

I think the reason for this is that *law-abiding citizens* are the backbone of any society. When people abide by the laws, it helps maintain social order, fosters a sense of security, and promotes trust in the government and legal system.

我认为这是因为守法公民（law-abiding citizens）是社会的重要支柱。人们遵守法律有助于维护社会秩序，培养安全感，以及增进对政府和法律体系的信任。

02 act in the public interest

该短语的意思相当于"代表公众利益",比如：He claimed to be acting in the public interest. 他声称自己代表的是公众利益。同时,be in the public interest 也是一个常用表达,意思是"符合公众利益",比如：a policy that is not in the public interest 意为"一项不符合公众利益的政策"。

What role do you think the government should play in society?
你认为政府在社会中应该扮演什么样的角色?

I think the government should *act in the public interest* and provide essential services to its citizens. For example, it should provide healthcare, education, and infrastructure to ensure that everyone has access to basic necessities. Additionally, it should regulate industries to ensure that they are not harming the environment or exploiting workers.

我认为政府应该代表公共利益（act in the public interest）,为公民提供基本服务。例如,政府应提供医疗保健、教育和基础设施,确保每个人都能获得基本必需品。此外,政府还应该对各行各业进行监管,确保它们不会破坏环境或剥削工人。

03 make the public aware of something

用法解析

make somebody aware of something 的意思是"让某人意识到某事物",比如:We need to make people more aware of these problems. 我们需要让人更加意识到这些问题。短语 make the public aware of something 即"让公众意识到某事"。

实用语境

What do you think are the responsibilities of a government?
你认为政府都有哪些责任?

I think the main responsibility of a government is to ensure that its citizens are safe and have access to basic necessities such as food, water, and shelter. The government should also be responsible for launching public awareness campaigns to educate people about important issues such as climate change, health, and safety. For example, the government should *make the public aware of* the importance of leading an active lifestyle.

我认为,政府的主要职责是确保公民的安全,使他们能够获得食物、水和住所等基本必需品。政府还应该负责开展公共宣传活动,向人们宣传气候变化、健康和安全等重要问题。例如,政府应让公众认识到(make the public aware of)积极生活方式的重要性。

04 increase police presence

该短语中的 presence 意思是"（观察控制形势的）一队警察或部队"，比如：Soldiers still maintain a military presence in the area. 士兵们仍然驻守在该地区。短语 increase police presence 的意思即"增加警力"。

用法解析

What measures can be taken to reduce crime rates? 可以采取哪些措施来降低犯罪率？

实用语境

I think one of the most effective measures is to *increase police presence* in high-crime areas. This can help to deter criminals from committing crimes in these areas. Additionally, it's important to provide marginalized groups with more support, such as counseling and job training programs. By addressing the root causes of crime, we can help to prevent it from happening in the first place.

我认为最有效的措施之一是在犯罪高发区增加警力（increase police presence）。这有助于阻止罪犯在这些地区犯罪。此外，为社会边缘群体提供更多支持也很重要，这些支持包括心理咨询和就业培训计划。通过解决犯罪的根本原因，我们可以从一开始就防止犯罪的发生。

05 make amends for somebody's crimes

 用法解析

make amends for something 的意思是"补偿某事带来的伤害",比如: He wanted to make amends for causing their marriage to fail. 他导致了他们的婚姻破裂,因此想做出补偿。短语 make amends for somebody's crimes 即"为某人曾经犯下的罪行做补偿",这是犯罪类话题中的常见表达。

 实用语境

Do you think community correction in the US can be an effective alternative to prison sentences?
你认为社区矫正在美国可以有效替代监狱服刑吗?

Yes, I do think so. Community correction in the US not only helps to reduce overcrowding in prisons, but also allows offenders to *make amends for* their crimes by giving back to their communities. Additionally, community correction can help offenders develop new skills and gain valuable work experience, which can make it easier for them to find employment after they have completed their sentence.

是的,我确实这么认为。社区矫正在美国不仅有助于缓解监狱人满为患的状况,还能让罪犯通过回馈社区来弥补自己的罪行(make amends for their crimes)。此外,社区矫正还可以帮助罪犯发展新的技能,获得宝贵的工作经验,从而使他们在刑满释放后更容易找到工作。

06 change somebody's ways

change somebody's ways 是一个固定搭配，意思相当 于 somebody behaves much better，即"某人改过自 新"。比如：Greg has really changed his ways since he went to prison. 格雷格入狱后真的改过自新了。

用法解析

What do you think about rehabilitation programs? 你如何看待犯人改造项目？

实用语境

I believe that rehabilitation programs are very important because they can help people who have committed crimes to *change their ways* and become a better person. For example, if someone has a drug addiction and they commit a crime to support their habit, then rehabilitation can help them to overcome their addiction and get their life back on track.

我认为犯人改造项目非常重要，因为它们可以帮 助罪犯改过自新（change their ways），成为一个 更好的人。例如，如果某人有毒瘾，并通过犯罪 来维持毒瘾，那么改造可以帮助他们克服毒瘾， 让生活重回正轨。

07 be high on the government's agenda

用法解析

agenda 的意思是"日程表"。Something is high on the government's agenda 的意思是"某事在政府日程表中排名靠前",引申为"某事是政府重点关注的议题"。

实用语境

What are some of the key societal challenges you think governments should address?
你认为政府应该应对哪些重大的社会挑战?

One challenge that should be *high on the government's agenda* is income inequality. The gap between the rich and the poor is widening, which can lead to various negative consequences, including high crime rates and slower economic growth. Another pressing issue is climate change. The government needs to take action to reduce greenhouse gas emissions, promote renewable energy, and protect natural resources.

收入不平等是政府应高度重视的一项挑战（high on the government's agenda）。贫富差距不断扩大，可能导致各种负面影响，包括犯罪率高和经济增长放缓。另一个紧迫问题是气候变化。政府需要采取行动，减少温室气体排放，推广可再生能源，保护自然资源。

08 the public purse

purse 的意思是"钱包", the public purse 即"公共钱包", 引申为"公共财政, 政府经费", 比如: Having a lot of people out of work places a large drain on the public purse. 大量人口失业使政府的财力消耗很大。

What are some of the challenges that governments face when managing their finances?
政府在财政管理方面面临哪些挑战?

I think one of the biggest challenges that governments face when managing *the public purse* is balancing competing priorities. For example, they may need to decide whether to invest in infrastructure projects or social programs. Another challenge is ensuring that public funds are not wasted or misused, which requires strong oversight and accountability mechanisms.

我认为, 政府在管理公共财政 (the public purse) 时面临的最大挑战之一就是要平衡各个项目的优先级。例如, 他们可能需要决定是投资基础设施项目还是社会项目。另一个挑战是确保公共资金不被浪费或滥用, 这需要强有力的监督和问责机制。

09 improve social mobility

用法解析

social mobility 的意思是"社会阶层流动性",要表达"教育是提高社会阶层的关键",可以说:Education is the key to upward social mobility. 短语 improve social mobility 即"提升社会阶层流动性"。

实用语境

What do you think are the most important roles of the government?
你认为政府最重要的职责都有哪些?

Firstly, I believe that the government has a crucial role to play in *improving social mobility*. By providing access to education and training, the government can help people from all backgrounds to achieve their full potential and contribute to society. Additionally, the government should help to create a fairer society by ensuring that everyone has access to basic services such as healthcare and housing. Finally, the government should protect citizens from harm, which can be achieved by providing a strong police force and an effective legal system.

首先,我相信政府在提高社会阶层流动性(improve social mobility)方面可以发挥至关重要的作用。通过提供教育和培训机会,政府可以帮助各种背景的人充分发挥潜能,为社会做贡献。此外,政府应确保人人都能获得医疗保健和住房等基本服务,从而帮助创建一个更加公平的社会。最后,政府应保护公民免受伤害,这可以通过提供强大的警力和有效的法律体系来实现。

10 reintegrate into society

reintegrate into society 的意思是"回归社会",注意 泛指"社会"时要说 society,而不是 the society。短 语用法是 help somebody reintegrate into society 或 者 reintegrate somebody into society。

 用法解析

Do you think young criminals in the US should be sent to prison for serious crimes?
你认为应该将犯有严重罪行的年轻罪犯送进监狱 吗?

 实用语境

No, I don't think so. Prison is a very harsh environment in the US, where young offenders can be exposed to violence and abuse from other inmates. Sending young offenders to prison also takes away their opportunity to receive education, which will make it harder for them to *reintegrate into society* after their release. Prison will not help them reform, but rather make them more likely to reoffend in the future.

不,我不这么认为。美国监狱是一个非常严酷的 环境,在那里,青少年罪犯可能会遭受其他囚犯 的暴力和虐待。将青少年罪犯送进监狱还剥夺了 他们接受教育的机会,这将使他们在出狱后更难 重新融入社会(reintegrate into society)。监狱不 会帮助他们改过自新,反而会使他们在将来更有 可能重新犯罪。

11 | abuse somebody's power

用法解析

abuse 在这里的意思不是"虐待",而是"滥用,妄用",比如:She is continually abusing her position by getting other people to do things for her. 她不断滥用职权让别人替她做事。短语 abuse somebody's power 即"某人滥用权力"。

实用语境

What qualities should a police officer have?
警察应具备哪些素质?

I think police officers should be honest and fair in enforcing the law and dealing with people, without *abusing their power* or taking bribes. They should also be professional and competent in their duties, and follow the rules and regulations of their organization. Moreover, a police officer should have compassion and empathy for the people they encounter, especially the victims of crime or violence, and try to help them as much as possible.

我认为,警察在执法和待人接物时应廉洁公正,不滥用权力(abuse their power),不收受贿赂。他们还应该专业、称职地履行职责,并遵守所在组织的规章制度。此外,警务人员应对所遇到的人抱有怜悯和同情之心(尤其是对犯罪或暴力的受害者),并尽量帮助他们。

12 provide financial incentives to something

financial incentives 的意思是"财政奖励"，短语 provide financial incentives to something 含义是 "向……提供财政奖励"，政府通过提供财政奖励可以 鼓励个人和企业做很多事情，比如保护环境、减少浪费 以及进行技术创新等。

用法解析

How can the government reduce the unemployment rate?
政府应该如何减少失业率？

实用语境

I think there are several measures the government can take to tackle unemployment. One way is to invest in education programs to upskill the workforce. This enables people to find better job opportunities and align their skills with the changing job market demands. Additionally, *providing financial incentives to* small- and medium-sized enterprises can help to create jobs. The government can also implement flexible labor market policies, which may encourage companies to expand and hire more workers.

我认为政府可以采取几种措施来解决失业问题。 方法之一是投资教育项目以提高劳动者的技能。 这能让人们找到更好的工作机会，使他们的技能 符合不断变化的就业市场需求。此外，为中小型 企业提供财政激励（provide financial incentives）措 施也有助于创造就业机会。政府还可以实施灵活 的劳动力市场政策，鼓励企业扩大规模，雇用更 多员工。

13 | provide a safety net for somebody

用法解析

safety net 原本的意思是"（保护高处表演者的）安全网，防护网"，它引申为"（为面临重大困难且无助的人提供帮助的）安全网，保障机制"。短语 provide a safety net for somebody 即"为某人提供一个安全保障体系"，比如：The welfare state was set up to provide a safety net for the poor and needy. 建立福利制度以为穷人和有需要的人提供保障机制。

实用语境

How can the government help poor people?
政府应该如何帮助穷人？

One way the government can help people who are struggling financially is by *providing a safety net for* them, which could include programs such as unemployment benefits, food assistance, and housing subsidies. These programs can reduce inequality and help people get out of financial troubles.

政府帮助陷入经济困境的人的一种方式是为他们提供一个安全保障体系（provide a safety net），这一体系可能包括失业救济、食品援助和住房补贴等项目。这些项目可以减少不平等，帮助人们摆脱经济困境。

14 take care of the most vulnerable members of society

the most vulnerable members of society 即"社会中的弱势群体"，这些群体即我们常说的"老弱病残"。照顾好这些弱势群体也是政府的一个责任。

Do you think it's the responsibility of the government to help poor people?
你认为帮助穷人是政府的责任吗？

Yes, I think the government should be responsible for *taking care of the most vulnerable members of society*, and it has the resources and infrastructure to do so effectively. Of course, individuals also have a responsibility to work hard and try to improve their situation, but sometimes circumstances beyond their control can make this difficult. In these cases, it's important for the government to step in and provide support.

是的，我认为政府应该负责照顾社会中的弱势群体（take care of the most vulnerable members of society），而且政府有资源和基础设施来有效地做到这一点。当然，个人也有责任努力工作，尝试改善自己的处境，但有时外界不可抗力会使他们难以做到这一点。在这种情况下，政府必须介入并提供支持。

15 a level playing field

用法解析

a level playing field 是一个固定短语，意思是"公平竞争的环境，机会均等的环境"，比如：We ask for a level playing field when we compete with foreign companies. 我们寻求一个能与外国公司公平竞争的环境。要表达"创造一个公平竞争的环境"，可以说 level the playing field。

实用语境

How do you think the government can promote economic growth?
你认为政府应该如何促进经济增长？

I think one way the government can stimulate economic growth is by investing in infrastructure, such as roads, bridges, and public transportation, which can help to improve connectivity and facilitate trade. Another way is by providing tax breaks and subsidies for businesses to invest and create jobs. Additionally, the government can help to create *a level playing field* by enforcing fair competition laws and regulations, which can encourage innovation and entrepreneurship.

我认为政府刺激经济增长的一个方法是投资基础设施，如道路、桥梁和公共交通，这有助于提升交通和促进贸易。另一种方法是为企业投资和创造就业提供税收减免和补贴。此外，政府还可以通过执行公平竞争的法律法规，帮助创造公平的竞争环境（a level playing field），从而鼓励创新和创业。

16 limit the marketing of junk food to children

该短语的意思是"限制向儿童推销垃圾食品"，在涉及政府与公众健康话题时经常会用到该表达，比如：Governments should enact policies to limit the marketing of junk food to children in order to combat the rising rates of childhood obesity. 各国政府应制定政策，限制向儿童推销垃圾食品，以应对儿童肥胖率不断上升的问题。

Do you think governments should regulate what people eat?
你认为政府应该对人们的饮食进行监督吗？

That's a complex issue. While it's important for governments to promote healthy eating habits through education and public health initiatives, I believe individuals should ultimately have the freedom to choose their own diet. However, regulations could be useful in certain scenarios, such as *limiting the marketing of junk food to children* or ensuring food safety standards are met.

这是一个复杂的问题。虽然政府通过教育和公共卫生活动来推广健康饮食习惯很重要，但我认为个人最终应该有选择自己饮食的自由。不过，在某些情况下，监管是有用的，比如限制向儿童推销垃圾食品（limit the marketing of junk food to children）或确保食品符合安全标准。

17 drunk driving

 用法解析

drunk driving 的意思是"酒后驾车",也可以说成 drink-driving,其他常见的交通违法行为还有:speeding(超速),texting while driving(边开车边打字),running red lights(闯红灯)等。

 实用语境

How can we improve road safety in cities?
我们应该如何提升城市道路安全?

There are several ways to improve road safety. Firstly, strict enforcement of traffic rules is essential. Penalties for violations like speeding, *drunk driving*, and not wearing seat belts should be severe enough to deter people from breaking the rules. Secondly, improving infrastructure can also enhance safety. This includes better road design, adequate signage, and proper street lighting.

改善道路安全有几种方法。首先,必须严格执行交通规则。对超速行驶、酒后驾车(drunk driving)、不系安全带等违规行为的处罚应足够严厉,以震慑人们不敢违规。其次,改善基础设施也能提高安全性。这包括更好的道路设计、足够的标志和适当的街道照明。

18 foster a spirit of camaraderie and unity among nations

camaraderie 的意思是"同志情谊，友情"，比如：
the camaraderie of the women's basketball team 女
子篮球队的队友情谊。foster a spirit of camaraderie
and unity among nations 的意思是"培养国家之间的
友爱和团结精神"，在涉及国际合作话题时可以用上该
表达。

Can you explain the significance of international
sports events?
你能阐述一下国际体育赛事的意义吗?

Absolutely. International sports events are significant
as they *foster a spirit of camaraderie and unity* among
nations. They provide a platform for athletes to
represent their countries and compete at the highest
level. These events also promote cultural exchange
and mutual understanding among different nations.

当然可以。国际体育赛事意义重大，因为它们促
进了各国之间的友谊和团结精神（foster a spirit of
camaraderie and unity）。它们为运动员提供了一个
平台，让他们能代表自己的国家参加最高水平的
比赛。这些赛事还促进了不同国家之间的文化交
流和相互理解。

扫一扫，听录音

个人品质

Part
9

01 shy away from something
02 step out of your comfort zone
03 bounce back from failures
04 build resilience
05 take on challenges
06 contribute to society
07 exert oneself
08 open yourself up to something
09 navigate challenges
10 make the most of something
11 expand somebody's social circle
12 put your shoulder to the wheel
13 a positive outlook on life

01 shy away from something

用法解析

shy 在这里不是"害羞"的意思，而是"逃避"，shy away from challenges/responsibilities 即"逃避挑战／责任"。

实用语境

How do you think people can develop their confidence?
你认为人们应该如何提升自信？

I think one way to develop confidence is by facing challenges head-on. When we *shy away from* challenges, we miss out on opportunities to learn and grow. By taking on challenges and finding a solution to them, we can gain valuable experience and build our self-confidence.

我认为培养自信的方法之一就是直面挑战。当我们回避（shy away from）挑战时，就会错失学习和成长的机会。通过接受挑战并找到解决方法，我们可以获得宝贵的经验并建立自信。

02 step out of your comfort zone

step out of your comfort zone 即我们常说的"走出
舒适区",比如：Starting a new business requires
entrepreneurs to step out of their comfort zone and
take risks. 创办一家新企业需要创业者走出自己的舒适
区并承担风险。

What do you think about taking risks?
你如何看待冒险？

I think taking risks is important because it helps us
grow. When we *step out of our comfort zone*, we learn
new things and gain new experiences. For example,
when I decided to study abroad, I was nervous about
leaving my family and friends behind, but I knew I
had to challenge myself. It turned out I was right. I
learned a lot about different cultures and gained a
new perspective on life.

我认为冒险很重要，因为它有助于我们成长。当我
们走出舒适区时（step out of our comfort zone），
我们会学到新东西，获得新体验。例如，当我决
定出国留学时，我对离开家人和朋友感到紧张，
但我知道我必须挑战自己。事实证明我是对的。
我学到了很多关于不同文化的知识，对生活有了
新的认识。

03 | bounce back from failures

用法解析

bounce 作为动词可以表示"反弹，弹起"，bounce back 可以引申为"恢复元气，重振旗鼓"，短语 bounce back from failures 可以理解为"失败之后东山再起"。

实用语境

What do you think are the main factors that contribute to a person's success in life?
你认为决定一个人成功的主要因素是什么？

I believe that factors such as talent, education, and hard work all play a part in a person's success. But I think the most important factor is the ability to *bounce back from failures*. Successful people are not afraid of making mistakes or facing challenges. They learn from their failures and use them as opportunities to improve themselves.

我认为天赋、教育和勤奋等因素都会对一个人的成功产生影响。但我认为最重要的因素是失败后东山再起（bounce back from failures）的能力。成功人士不怕犯错，也不怕面对挑战。他们从失败中吸取教训，并将其作为提升自我的机会。

04 build resilience

resilience 的意思相当于"适应能力"，比如：She has shown great resilience to stress. 她对压力表现出了极大的适应能力。短语 build resilience 即"建立适应能力"。

Is failure important in one's personal and professional development?
失败经历对个人和职业发展重要吗？

Absolutely. I believe that failure is an essential part of personal and professional growth. It provides us with valuable lessons and opportunities for improvement. When we encounter failure, we have a chance to reflect on our actions, identify our weaknesses, and learn from our mistakes. It helps us *build resilience* and perseverance, which are crucial traits for success in any aspect of life.

当然。我认为失败是个人和职业成长的重要组成部分。它为我们提供了宝贵的经验教训和改进机会。遇到失败时，我们有机会反思自己的行为，找出自己的弱点，并从错误中吸取教训。它能帮助我们建立韧性和毅力（build resilience），这是在生活的任何方面取得成功的关键特质。

05 take on challenges

take on challenges 的意思是"接受挑战",比如:
The new headteacher has taken on the challenge of improving the school. 新校长接受了改进学校的挑战。

How can people overcome the fear of failure?
人们如何克服对失败的恐惧?

To overcome the fear of failure, it's essential to adopt a positive mindset and embrace failures as learning experiences. Accepting that failure is a part of the journey towards growth can help people *take on new challenges*. Setting realistic goals and breaking them down into smaller achievable tasks can also make the process less daunting.

要克服对失败的恐惧,就必须采取积极的心态,把失败当作学习的经历。接受失败是成长旅程的一部分,这有助于人们接受新的挑战(take on new challenges)。制订切实可行的目标,并将其分解为可实现的小任务,这也能让实现目标的过程不再令人生畏。

06 contribute to society

contribute to society 即我们常说的"为社会做出贡献"，比如纳税、做慈善以及保护环境等。注意泛指"社会"时直接用 society，前面不用加定冠词 the。

In what areas of life do you think people should take more responsibility?
你认为人们应该在哪些领域中承担更多责任？

Firstly, people should take responsibility for their health by adopting a healthy lifestyle. Secondly, they should take responsibility for their work and actions, which can lead to a more productive and friendly work environment. Finally, I think people have a responsibility to *contribute to society* in a positive way. This can be achieved through volunteering or embracing eco-friendly practices.

首先，人们应该对自己的健康负责，要采取健康的生活方式。其次，人们应该对自己的工作和行为负责，这样才能创造一个更有效率、更友好的工作环境。最后，我认为人们有责任以积极的方式为社会做出贡献（contribute to society）。这可以通过志愿服务或环保实践来实现。

07 exert oneself

用法解析

exert oneself 的意思相当于"付出很大努力"，该短语可以用来代替常见说法 work hard。比如：In order to be successful, he would have to exert himself. 他必须努力才能成功。

实用语境

Do you think it is important to set goals?
你认为设立目标重要吗？

Yes, I believe that setting goals is of great importance because it gives us a clear direction and something to strive for. When we have a goal in mind, we are more likely to *exert ourselves* and work towards achieving it, which can lead to personal growth.

是的，我认为制定目标非常重要，因为它给了我们一个明确的方向和奋斗目标。当我们心中有了目标，就更有可能努力奋斗（exert ourselves）去实现目标，从而实现个人成长。

08 open yourself up to something

该短语的意思相当于"让自己主动接触到某事"，比如 open yourself up to new possibilities/ new opportunities/ the unknown（获得新的可能 / 新机会 / 未知的事）。

用法解析

Do you think people should take risks in order to grow personally?
你认为人们应该为了个人成长而承担风险吗？

实用语境

Yes, I believe that taking risks is an important part of personal growth. When we step outside of our comfort zone and try new things, we *open ourselves up to* new experiences and opportunities. Of course, taking risks also means that we might fail, but failure can be a valuable learning experience. By taking calculated risks and being willing to learn from our mistakes, we can continue to grow personally.

是的，我认为冒险是个人成长的重要组成部分。当我们走出舒适区，尝试新事物时，我们能够获得（open ourselves up to）新的体验和机会。当然，冒险也意味着我们可能会失败，但失败也可以成为宝贵的学习经验。通过承担一定的风险并愿意从错误中吸取教训，我们可以不断实现个人成长。

09 navigate challenges

用法解析

navigate 除了可以表示"导航，确定……的方向"之外，还可以指"理解，应对（困难复杂的情况）"，比如：A solicitor will help you navigate the complex legal system. 会有一位律师来帮助你应对错综复杂的司法制度。navigate challenges 即"应对挑战"。

实用语境

Do you think it's important to have a mentor or role model?
你认为导师或榜样重要吗？

Yes, I believe that having a mentor or role model is important. A mentor can provide guidance, support, and advice based on their own experiences. They can help us *navigate challenges* and overcome obstacles. Similarly, a role model can inspire us to strive for greatness and achieve our goals. Seeing someone who has achieved success in an area we are interested in can motivate us to work hard and persevere.

是的，我认为拥有一位导师或榜样是很重要的。导师可以根据自己的经验提供指导、支持和建议。他们可以帮助我们应对挑战（navigate challenges），克服困难。同样，榜样也能激励我们奋发图强，实现自己的目标。看到其他人在我们感兴趣的领域取得成功，可以激励我们努力工作，坚持不懈。

10 make the most of something

make the most of something 的意思是"最大限度地利用好某事物"，比如：Make the most of your time. 充分利用好你的时间。要表达"幸福就是有能力充分享受你拥有的一切"，可以说：Happiness is the ability to make the most of what you have.

用法解析

Do you think time management is important in today's fast-paced world?
你认为时间管理在当今快节奏的世界中重要吗？

实用语境

Yes, I think time management is extremely important in today's world. With the increasing demands of work, studies, and personal commitments, effectively managing our time allows us to *make the most of* every day. It helps us achieve our goals, reduce stress, and maintain a healthy work-life balance.

是的，我认为时间管理在当今世界极其重要。随着工作、学习和个人事务的要求越来越多，有效管理时间能让我们充分利用（make the most of）每一天。它能帮助我们实现目标，减轻压力，保持健康的工作生活平衡。

11 expand somebody's social circle

用法解析

expand somebody's social circle 的意思为"扩大某人的社交圈"，同义表达还有 widen somebody's circle of friends。

实用语境

Do you think it's important for people to have hobbies?
你认为人拥有爱好重要吗？

Yes, I do think so. Having hobbies is crucial for maintaining a balanced lifestyle. Hobbies offer a way to escape the daily stress and routine. They also help people develop new skills and interests outside of their work or studies. Moreover, hobbies can foster a sense of community and help people *expand their social circle*, as they provide opportunities to meet like-minded people and build meaningful connections.

是的，我是这么认为的。拥有爱好对于保持平衡的生活方式至关重要。业余爱好为人们提供了一种避开日常压力的方式。业余爱好还能帮助人们发展工作或学习之外的新技能和新兴趣。此外，业余爱好还可以培养团体归属感，帮助人们扩大社交圈（expand their social circle），因为它们提供了结识志同道合者和建立有意义连接的机会。

12 put your shoulder to the wheel

put your shoulder to the wheel 的字面意思是"在
推动机器轮子时将肩膀放在轮子上（以便更好出
力）"，引申为：to start to work with great effort
and determination，即"全力以赴（做某事）"。

用法解析

What are some effective ways for people to achieve
their goals?
人们实现目标的有效途径有哪些?

实用语境

There are many effective ways for people to reach
their goals. One way is to break down larger goals into
smaller, more manageable steps. This can help people
stay motivated and make progress towards their
goals. Another way is to seek support and guidance
from others, such as a mentor or coach. Finally, it's
important for people to *put their shoulders to the
wheel* to attain their goals.

人们实现目标的有效方法有很多。其中一种方法
是将较大的目标分解成更小、更易于管理的步
骤。这可以帮助人们保持动力，朝着目标前进。
另一种方法是寻求他人的支持和指导，如导师或
教练。最后，重要的是人们要全力以赴（put their
shoulders to the wheel）去实现目标。

13 a positive outlook on life

用法解析

outlook 在这里的意思相当于 your general attitude to life and the world，即"（对生活和世界的）看法，观点，态度"，短语 a positive outlook on life 的意思是"积极的生活态度"。

实用语境

How important do you think optimism is in today's world?
你认为乐观主义在当今世界有多重要？

I believe that optimism plays a crucial role in today's world. It's not just about having *a positive outlook on life*, but also about having a powerful mindset that can shape our actions and decisions. Maintaining an optimistic attitude can help us stay motivated and resilient in the face of challenges.

我认为乐观主义在当今世界发挥着至关重要的作用。它不仅关乎积极的人生观（a positive outlook on life），还关乎强大的心态，这种心态能够影响我们的行动和决策。保持乐观的态度可以帮助我们在面对挑战时保持动力和韧性。

扫一扫，听录音

Part 10

文化话题

01   connect with your roots

02   something provides a window into the past

03   something is passed down from generation to generation

04   something is steeped in history

05   something brings history to life

06   something is a means of self-expression

07   keep traditions alive

08   something is an important part of our culture and heritage

09   make way for new developments

10   something provides a tangible link to the past

11   bring people together

12   something holds a special place in people's hearts

13   blend traditional elements with modern fashion trends

14   expose somebody to something

15   something is a universal language

16   something is architecturally significant

17   wear and tear

18   something offers insights into...

19   draw inspiration from something

20   something carries historical and architectural significance

21   a hands-on learning experience

22   something weakens the social fabric of a country

23   the homogenization of cultures

24   immerse yourself in something

25   resonate with somebody

26   somebody becomes assimilated into the community

27   a personal touch

01 | connect with your roots

用法解析

roots 在这里指"某人的根，某人与家乡的情感联系"，connect with your roots 的意思相当于"与自己的根联系起来，寻根"。这一表达在涉及传统文化的话题中经常出现。

实用语境

How important is traditional clothing in your culture?
传统服饰在你们文化中的重要性如何？

Traditional clothing holds significant importance in my culture. It's not just a way of dressing; it's also a representation of our heritage, values, and history. People often wear traditional clothes during festivals, weddings, and other special occasions to *connect with their roots* and showcase their cultural pride.

传统服装在我们国家的文化中具有重要意义。它不仅是一种着装方式，还代表着我们的传统、价值观和历史。人们经常在节日、婚礼和其他特殊场合穿着传统服装，这样做能与自己的根源联系在一起（connect with their roots），并展示自己的文化自豪感。

02 something provides a window into the past

该表达的意思是"某事物提供了一个了解过去的窗口"。 用法解析
举个例子，博物馆、传统习俗、文学作品以及古建筑
都能为人们提供了解过去的窗口。该短语也可以说成
provide a glimpse into the past。

Do you think the museum is important? 实用语境
你认为博物馆重要吗？

Yes, I think museums are extremely important because
they serve as repositories of our cultural heritage,
preserving and presenting historical artifacts that
allow us to connect with our roots and understand
our history. By *providing a window into* the past,
museums also offer valuable educational experiences
and help us appreciate the accomplishments and
struggles of our ancestors.

是的，我认为博物馆极其重要，因为它们是我们
文化遗产的宝库，能够保存和展示历史文物。这
些文物让我们与我们的根源联系起来，并且让我
们对历史有所了解。通过提供一个了解过去的窗
口（provide a window into the past），博物馆还提
供了宝贵的教育经验，帮助我们理解祖先的成就
和奋斗。

03 something is passed down from generation to generation

用法解析

该表达的意思是"某事物被代代相传"，我们可以用它来形容艺术品、传统习俗以及价值观等。它也可以说成 Something is passed down from one generation to the next。

实用语境

Why is it important to protect cultural heritage?
为什么保护文化遗产很重要？

I think the reason why people should protect their cultural heritage is that it encompasses traditions, customs, arts and values that have been *passed down from generation to generation*. It connects them to their roots and shapes their identity, so it is important that people protect and pay homage to their cultural heritage.

我认为人们之所以应该保护自己的文化遗产，是因为它包含了代代相传的（passed down from generation to generation）传统、习俗、艺术和价值观。它将人们与自己的根源联系在一起，并塑造了他们的身份。因此，人们必须保护并向他们的文化遗产致敬。

04 something is steeped in history

something is steeped in history 的意思是"某事物历史悠久",比如: a town that is steeped in history 历史悠久的小城。该表达通常用于描述某个地方历史文化源远流长。

What kind of places do you like to visit?
你喜欢参观哪一类地方?

I'm really interested in visiting places that are *steeped in history*. For example, I recently visited the ancient city of Athens. It was amazing to see how people lived thousands of years ago and how they built such incredible structures.

我非常喜欢游览历史悠久的地方(be steeped in history)。例如,我最近参观了雅典古城。看到几千年前的人们如何生活以及他们如何建造出如此让人难以置信的建筑,真是令人惊叹。

05 | something brings history to life

用法解析

该表达的意思是"某事物让历史以更加生动的方式呈现出来"。博物馆、古城以及传统艺术都能以更加生动的方式来呈现历史。比如：Museums and historical sites bring history to life, allowing visitors to experience the past in a tangible way. 博物馆和历史遗址让历史栩栩如生，让参观者以直观的形式感受过去。

实用语境

What are your favorite historical places?
你最喜欢哪些历史景点？

I love old buildings and museums. They are like time capsules that *bring history to life*. I visited the Tower of London last year and it was amazing. The tour guide was very knowledgeable and passionate about the history of the place. I learned so much from her.

我喜欢参观古建筑和博物馆。它们就像时间胶囊，让历史以更加生动的方式呈现出来（bring history to life）。去年我参观了伦敦塔，感觉非常棒。导游知识渊博，对那里的历史充满热情。我从她那里学到了很多东西。

06 something is a means of self-expression

该表达的意思是"某事物是一种自我表达的方式"，比如绘画、音乐和雕塑这些艺术品就是艺术家一种自我表达的方式。

用法解析

Do you think art is important in our society?
你认为艺术在我们社会中重要吗？

实用语境

Yes, I do think so. Art is not only a form of entertainment, but also *a means of self-expression*. It can convey emotions and ideas that words cannot always express. For example, through art, artists are able to convey universal human experiences and emotions without the limitations of language or cultural barriers.

是的，我是这样认为的。艺术不仅是一种娱乐形式，也是一种自我表达的手段（a means of self-expression）。它可以传达语言无法表达的情感和思想。例如，艺术家能够通过艺术传达人类的普遍经验和情感，而不受语言或文化障碍的限制。

07 keep traditions alive

用法解析

keep traditions alive 的意思相当于"保留传统，让传统继续存在"，它可以替代常见说法 preserve traditions。

实用语境

In what ways does traditional music contribute to preserving cultural identity?
传统音乐在哪些方面能够保护文化特性？

Traditional music acts as a powerful bridge to our cultural roots. It carries stories, emotions, and values that are deeply embedded in our history. By listening to and performing traditional music, we *keep our traditions alive* and pass them on to future generations. It's a way to ensure that our cultural identity isn't lost amidst the wave of globalization.

传统音乐是通往我们文化根源的桥梁。它承载着深植于我们历史中的故事、情感和价值观。通过聆听和演奏传统音乐，我们可以保留我们的传统（keep our traditions alive），并将其传承给后代。这是确保我们的文化身份不会在全球化浪潮中消失的一种方式。

08 something is an important part of our culture and heritage

该表达的意思是"某事物是我们文化和传统的重要组成部分"，这是一个文化话题里面的万能表达。我们可以用它来描述古建筑、民间技艺、传统习俗以及传统美食等。

 用法解析

Why is it important to protect traditions?
为什么保护传统很重要?

 实用语境

It is important to protect traditions because they are *an important part of our culture and heritage*. They help us to connect with our past and understand where we come from. They also give us a sense of identity and belonging. So we should keep our traditions alive.

保护传统非常重要，因为它们是我们文化和遗产的重要组成部分（an important part of our culture and heritage）。它们帮助我们与过去建立联系，了解我们从哪里来。它们还赋予我们认同感和归属感。因此，我们应该保留我们的传统。

09 | make way for new developments

 用法解析

该短语中的 development 不是指"发展"，而是指"新建住宅区，新开发区"，make way for new developments 即"为新建住宅区或开发区让路"。在涉及古建筑保护的话题中经常会用到该表达。

 实用语境

What do you think should be done with old buildings that are no longer in use?
你认为应如何处理不再使用的旧建筑？

I think one option is to renovate old buildings and repurpose them for a new use, such as turning an old factory into a museum or art gallery. Another option is to preserve them as historical landmarks for people to visit and learn about the past. In some cases, it may be necessary to demolish old buildings to *make way for new developments* if they are unsafe or beyond repair, but I believe this should be a last resort.

我认为一种选择是翻新旧建筑，将它们用于新的用途，例如将旧工厂改造成博物馆或艺术馆。另一种办法是将它们作为历史地标保存起来，供人们参观和了解过去。在某些情况下，如果旧建筑不安全或无法修复，可能有必要拆除它们，以便为新建住宅区或开发区让路（make way for new developments），但我认为这应该是最后的手段。

10 something provides a tangible link to the past

该表达的意思是"某事物提供了一个与过去的生动联系"，像古建筑、文物以及传统服饰都能提供这种与过去的联系，比如：Museums can provide a tangible link to the past by preserving and displaying artifacts that tell the story of human history and culture. 博物馆可以通过保存和展示文物来与过去建立有形联系，这些文物讲述了有关人类历史和文化的故事。

Do you think it's important to preserve old buildings?
你认为保护古建筑重要吗？

Yes, I think it's important to preserve old buildings because they *provide a tangible link to the past* and help us to understand our history and heritage. They also add character and charm to a city, making it a more interesting and attractive place to live and visit. Old buildings should be preserved whenever possible.

是的，我认为保护古建筑很重要，因为它们提供了与过去的直观联系（provide a tangible link to the past），并帮助我们了解历史和文化遗产。它们还能为城市增添特色和魅力，使其成为一个更有趣、更有吸引力的居住地和旅游地。只要有可能，我们就应该保护古建筑。

11 bring people together

用法解析

该短语的意思是"让人们团结起来，让人们聚在一起"。传统节日、传统习俗以及共同价值观都具有团结民众的作用。比如：Festivals and cultural events have the power to bring people together, as they celebrate shared traditions and values, and foster a sense of community. 节日和文化活动具有将人们聚集在一起的力量，因为它们庆祝共同的传统和价值观，并培养社区精神。

实用语境

Do you think it's important to preserve traditional festivals?

你认为保护传统节日重要吗？

Yes, I believe that it's crucial to preserve traditional festivals because they are an integral part of our cultural heritage. They also *bring people together* and strengthen social bonds. By celebrating traditional festivals, we can pass on our traditions and values to future generations.

是的，我认为保护传统节日至关重要，因为它们是我们文化遗产不可分割的一部分。传统节日还能将人们聚集在一起（bring people together），加强社会联系。通过庆祝传统节日，我们可以将我们的传统和价值观传承给子孙后代。

12 something holds a special place in people's hearts

该表达的意思是"某事物在人们心目中有特殊的地位"，可以用来描述各种与传统文化相关的事物，比如：Family traditions, such as holiday gatherings or annual vacations, hold a special place in people's hearts because they strengthen the bonds between family members. 像节日聚会或年度假期这样的家庭传统在人们心中有着特殊的地位，因为它们加强了家庭成员之间的联系。

用法解析

Do you think traditional festivals are losing their importance in modern society?
你认为传统节日在现代社会中是否逐渐失去其重要性？

实用语境

I don't think so. While it's true that some aspects of traditional festivals may have changed over time, they still *hold a special place in people's hearts*. In fact, many people look forward to celebrating traditional festivals with their families and friends every year. So I believe that traditional festivals will continue to be an important part of our culture for many years to come.

我不这么认为。虽然随着时间的推移，传统节日的某些方面可能确实发生了变化，但它们在人们心中仍然占据着特殊的位置（hold a special place in people's hearts）。事实上，许多人每年都期待着与家人和朋友一起庆祝传统节日。因此，我相信在未来的许多年里，传统节日仍将是我们文化的重要组成部分。

13 blend traditional elements with modern fashion trends

用法解析

该短语的意思是"将传统元素与时尚潮流结合起来"，在描述服饰等潮流文化时可以用上该表达。

实用语境

Do you think young people in your country are still interested in wearing traditional clothing?
你认为你们国家的年轻人还喜欢穿传统服装吗？

Absolutely. While there's a growing influence of Western fashion, many young people in China still take pride in wearing traditional clothing. They often find creative ways to *blend traditional elements with modern fashion trends*, creating a unique fusion that resonates with their generation. Traditional clothing is also becoming a symbol of cultural identity for the youth, especially during cultural events and ceremonies.

当然。虽然西方时尚的影响越来越大，但中国的许多年轻人仍然以穿传统服装为荣。他们经常找到创造性的方法，将传统元素与现代时尚潮流相融合（blend traditional elements with modern fashion trends），创造出能引起他们这一代人共鸣的独特组合。传统服装也逐渐成为年轻人文化身份的象征，尤其是在文化活动和仪式中。

14 expose somebody to something

expose somebody to something 的字面意思是"将某人暴露在某事物当中",它可以引申为"让某人接触到某事物"。比如: We want to expose the kids to as much art and culture as possible. 我们想让孩子们受到尽可能多的艺术和文化熏陶。

用法解析

What do you think are the benefits of traveling?
你认为旅游的好处有哪些?

实用语境

Traveling offers a multitude of benefits. On an individual level, it broadens one's horizons by *exposing them to* new cultures, languages, and ways of life. It also encourages personal growth and promotes adaptability. For society, travel promotes cultural exchange and understanding, which can lead to reduced prejudices and greater global harmony. Additionally, the tourism industry can contribute significantly to a country's economy, creating jobs and driving infrastructure development.

旅行有很多好处。就个人而言,旅行能让人接触到(expose somebody to something)新的文化、语言和生活方式,从而开阔视野。旅行还能促进个人成长,提高适应能力。对社会而言,旅游可以促进文化交流和理解,从而减少偏见,增进全球和谐。此外,旅游业还能为国家经济做出重大贡献,创造就业机会,推动基础设施建设。

15 something is a universal language

 用法解析

该表达的意思是"某事物是一种通用语言"，比如很多人认为音乐是一种通用语言，因为来自不同文化的人都能理解它。

 实用语境

How do you think music impacts society?
你认为音乐如何影响社会？

Well, music is *a universal language* that transcends cultural and linguistic barriers. It has the power to evoke emotions, bring people together, and even influence social and political movements. For instance, protest songs have historically been used to express dissent and call for change. Music can also shape popular culture and fashion trends, reflecting the values and attitudes of a society.

音乐是一种通用语言（a universal language），它能超越文化和语言障碍。音乐能够唤起人们的情感，将人们聚集在一起，甚至影响社会和政治运动。例如，抗议歌曲历来被用来表达异议和呼吁变革。音乐还能塑造流行文化和时尚趋势，反映一个社会的价值观和态度。

16 something is architecturally significant

该表达的意思是"某事物在建筑上具有重要价值"，我们可以用该表达来描述古建筑和古城的价值。

用法解析

Do you think it's important to preserve old buildings?
你认为保护古建筑重要吗？

实用语境

Yes, I believe that it's important to preserve old buildings because they are a part of our cultural heritage and history. They can also provide valuable insights into the past. Additionally, many old buildings are *architecturally significant* and visually appealing.

是的，我认为保护古建筑很重要，因为它们是我们文化遗产和历史的一部分。它们还能为了解过去提供有价值的见解。此外，许多古建筑都具有重要的建筑意义（architecturally significant）和视觉吸引力。

17 wear and tear

 用法解析

wear and tear 是一个固定搭配，意思是"磨损，损坏"，注意 tear 要读成 /teə/。在描述文物或者古建筑遭受的磨损时，就可以用上该表达。

 实用语境

Is tourism good for historic sites?
旅游业对历史景点有益处吗？

I think tourism can be a double-edged sword for historic sites. On the one hand, increased tourism can boost the local economy by creating jobs and generating revenue for businesses. On the other hand, overcrowding and irresponsible tourism practices can indeed lead to *wear and tear* on these delicate sites. It's essential to strike a balance between allowing access for visitors and implementing measures to protect and conserve the sites.

我认为旅游业对历史遗址来说是一把双刃剑。一方面，旅游业的发展可以创造就业机会，为企业带来收入，从而促进当地经济的发展。另一方面，过度拥挤和不负责任的旅游行为确实会对这些脆弱的遗址造成损坏（wear and tear）。在允许游客进入遗址和采取措施保护遗址之间取得平衡至关重要。

18 something offers insights into…

something offers insights into … 的意思是"某事物提供了对于……的深刻见解",比如:The book gives us fascinating insights into life in Mexico. 这本书生动地表现了墨西哥的生活。注意此处 insights 用的是复数形式。

Do you think traditional paintings are still important in today's world?
你认为传统绘画在当今世界是否仍然重要?

Yes. Although modern art forms like digital art are gaining prominence, I believe that traditional paintings still hold significant value. Traditional paintings often carry cultural and historical narratives that connect us to our roots. For instance, looking at an ancient painting can *offer insights into* the beliefs, lifestyles, and events of a particular time period.

是的。虽然数字艺术等现代艺术形式日益流行,但我认为传统绘画仍然具有重要价值。传统绘画往往承载着文化和历史故事,将我们与自己的根源联系在一起。例如,观察一幅古代绘画可以让我们了解(offer insights into)特定时期的信仰、生活方式和历史事件。

19 draw inspiration from something

draw inspiration from something 的意思是"从某事物中获得灵感",比如:She draws inspiration from mythology and folk stories. 她从神话和民间故事中汲取灵感。

Do you think traditional paintings have any impact on contemporary artists and their work?
你认为传统绘画对当代艺术家及其作品有影响吗?

Absolutely, traditional paintings can be a wellspring of inspiration for contemporary artists. Many modern artists *draw inspiration from* the techniques, themes, and emotions conveyed in traditional artworks. By studying traditional paintings, contemporary artists can learn about different styles, color palettes, and composition techniques that have stood the test of time. This can lead to the creation of innovative and unique artworks.

当然。传统绘画是当代艺术家的灵感源泉。许多现代艺术家从传统艺术作品的技法、主题和情感中汲取灵感(draw inspiration from)。通过研究传统绘画,当代艺术家可以学习不同的风格、调色板和构图技巧,这些东西都经历了时间的考验。这样就能创作出创新而独特的艺术作品。

20 something carries historical and architectural significance

用法解析

something carries historical and architectural significance 的意思为"某事物在历史和建筑上具有重要价值"。我们可以用该表达来描述古建筑和古城的重要性。

实用语境

What are some reasons for protecting old buildings?
保护古建筑的原因有哪些?

Preserving old buildings serves several important purposes. Firstly, old buildings often *carry historical and architectural significance*, reflecting the cultural identity and heritage of a place. By protecting them, we ensure that future generations can appreciate and learn about the past. Moreover, these buildings can attract tourists, contributing to the local economy.

保护古建筑有几个重要目的。首先,这些建筑往往具有历史和建筑意义(carry historical and architectural significance),反映了一个地方的文化特征和遗产。通过保护它们,我们可以确保子孙后代能够欣赏和了解过去。此外,这些建筑还能吸引游客,促进当地经济发展。

21 a hands-on learning experience

用法解析

该短语中的 hands-on 意思是"亲自实践的，实际操作的"，比如：Many employers consider hands-on experience to be as useful as academic qualifications. 很多雇主都认为实务经验和学历一样有用。a hands-on learning experience 意思是"亲身实践学习的经验"，比如参观博物馆和旅游都能够提供这样的经验。

实用语境

Do you think it's important for children to visit museums?
你认为儿童参观博物馆重要吗？

Yes, I think it's important for children to visit museums because they can provide *a hands-on learning experience* that complements classroom education. Interactive exhibits and workshops in the museum can spark children's curiosity and encourage them to explore various subjects, fostering a love for learning. Moreover, museums often offer specialized educational programs for schools, making learning outside the classroom more engaging and memorable.

是的，我认为儿童参观博物馆非常重要，因为博物馆可以提供实践学习体验（a hands-on learning experience），与课堂教育相辅相成。博物馆中的互动展品和工作坊可以激发孩子们的好奇心，鼓励他们探索各种主题，培养他们对学习的热爱。此外，博物馆还经常为学校提供专门的教育计划，使课堂外的学习更有吸引力，更令人难忘。

22 something weakens the social fabric of a country

social fabric 的意思是"社会结构", something weakens the social fabric of a country 相当于"某事物弱化了一个国家的社会结构", 比如传统文化习俗的消失以及方言的消失都会弱化社会结构。

How important do you think it is for a country to preserve and promote its minority languages?
你认为保护和推广小众语言对一个国家有多重要?

Preserving and promoting minority languages is crucial, because language is an integral part of a culture's identity. When minority languages are lost, a significant aspect of a community's heritage disappears. This can *weaken the social fabric of a country* and lead to a loss of cultural diversity.

我认为保护和推广小语种至关重要, 因为语言是文化身份不可分割的一部分。当小语种消失时, 社区遗产的一大部分也随之消失。这会削弱一个国家的社会结构(weaken the social fabric of a country), 导致文化多样性的丧失。

23 the homogenization of cultures

 用法解析

homogenization 的意思是"同质化，单一化"，the homogenization of cultures 即"文化的同质化"，可以用该表达来描述全球化和互联网带来的影响。

 实用语境

How do you think globalization has affected traditional cultures?
你认为全球化对传统文化有何影响？

Globalization has had a significant impact on traditional cultures. On the one hand, it has allowed for the spread of ideas and cultural exchange, which can help to preserve and promote traditional cultures. On the other hand, it has also led to *the homogenization of cultures*, where local traditions are threatened by outside influences.

全球化对传统文化产生了重大影响。一方面，全球化促进了思想的传播和文化的交流，有助于保护和发扬传统文化。另一方面，全球化也导致了文化的同质化（the homogenization of cultures），地方传统文化受到了外来影响的威胁。

24 immerse yourself in something

immerse yourself in something 表示"沉浸在某事物当中"，比如：She got some books out of the library and immersed herself in Chinese history and culture. 她从图书馆借了一些书，然后沉浸于中国历史和文化之中。

用法解析

What do you think are the benefits of cultural tourism? 你认为文化旅游有哪些优点？

实用语境

Cultural tourism can have many benefits. Firstly, it can help to preserve and promote local traditions and customs. It can also provide economic benefits to the local community by creating jobs and generating income for local people. Additionally, cultural tourism offers tourists an opportunity to *immerse themselves in* the local traditions, history, and way of life.

文化旅游有很多好处。首先，它有助于保护和促进当地的传统和习俗。它还可以为当地人创造就业机会和收入，从而为当地社区带来经济效益。此外，文化旅游还为游客提供了一个深度体验（immerse themselves in）当地传统、历史和生活方式的机会。

25 resonate with somebody

用法解析

resonate with somebody 的意思是"与某人产生共鸣"，比如：These issues resonated with the voters. 这些问题引起了投票者的共鸣。在描述音乐、绘画和诗歌等文艺作品的影响时经常可以用上该表达。

实用语境

How do you think pop culture influences young people?
你认为流行文化是如何影响年轻人的？

I believe that pop culture has a significant influence on young people. It shapes their tastes, preferences, and even their values. For example, popular music, movies, and TV shows often reflect the attitudes and beliefs of the time, and these messages tend to *resonate with* young people. They may adopt the fashion trends, language, and behaviors that they see in pop culture, and this can have a profound impact on their identity and self-expression.

我认为流行文化对年轻人有重大影响。它塑造了他们的品位、喜好甚至价值观。例如，流行音乐、电影和电视节目往往反映了当时的态度和信仰，而这些信息往往会引起年轻人的共鸣（resonate with）。他们可能会模仿在流行文化中看到的时尚潮流、语言和行为，这可能会对他们的身份认同和自我表达产生深远的影响。

26 somebody becomes assimilated into the community

该表达的意思是"某人融入了社区"，比如：Refugees find it difficult to become assimilated into the community. 难民发觉难以融入社区。在涉及移民类话题时经常可以用上该表达。

用法解析

How important is it for immigrants to learn about the culture of their new country?
对移民来说，了解新国家的文化有多重要？

实用语境

I believe that it is crucial for immigrants to learn about the culture of their new country. By understanding the customs, traditions, and values of their new community, immigrants can feel more comfortable in their new surroundings. This can reduce misunderstandings or conflicts that may arise from cultural differences, and help immigrants *become assimilated into the community*.

我认为了解新国家的文化对移民来说至关重要。通过了解新社区的习俗、传统和价值观，移民可以在新环境中感到更加舒适。这可以减少因文化差异而产生的误解或冲突，帮助移民融入社区（become assimilated into the community）。

27 | a personal touch

该短语中的 touch 意思为"风格，手法"，a personal touch 可以理解为"有个人风格的，有人情味的"，比如：Our staff combine efficient service with a personal touch. 我们的员工既有高效的服务，又有亲切的态度。

Why do you think some people prefer to buy handicrafts rather than mass-produced items?

你认为为什么有些人喜欢购买手工艺品而不是大规模生产的物品？

I think there are several reasons why people do this. Some people buy handicrafts because they appreciate the skill and effort that goes into making something by hand. They may also value *the personal touch* that comes with a handmade item. Additionally, buying handicrafts can support local artisans and help preserve traditional crafts and techniques. Overall, I think people who buy handicrafts are looking for something special and meaningful, rather than just another mass-produced item.

我认为人们这样做有几个原因。有些人购买手工艺品是因为他们欣赏手工制作过程中的技巧和努力。他们可能还看重手工制品所带来的人情味（the personal touch）。此外，购买手工艺品还可以支持当地工匠，帮助保护传统工艺和技术。总之，我认为购买手工艺品的人是在寻找特别的、有意义的东西，而不仅仅是另一种大规模生产的物品。